YOUNG WRITERS
Spellbound

WEST MIDLANDS

Edited by Simon Harwin

First published in Great Britain in 1998 by
POETRY NOW YOUNG WRITERS
1-2 Wainman Road, Woodston,
Peterborough, PE2 7BU
Telephone (01733) 230748

All Rights Reserved

Copyright Contributors 1998

HB ISBN 0 75430 020 X
SB ISBN 0 75430 021 8

FOREWORD

In this, our 5th competition year, we are proud to present *Spellbound West Midlands*. This anthology represents the very best endeavours of the children from this region.

The standard of entries was high, which made the task of editing a difficult one, but nonetheless enjoyable. The variety of subject matter, creativity and imagination never ceases to amaze and is indeed an inspiration to us all.

This year's competition attracted the highest entry ever - over 46,000 from all over the UK, and for the first time included entries from English speaking children living abroad.

Congratulations to all the writers published in *Spellbound West Midlands*. We hope you enjoy reading the poems and that your success will inspire you to continue writing in the future.

Contents

Debbie Harrison	1

Arden School

Alison Smith	2
Alix Windsor	3
Rebecca Thomas	4
Rachel Bromley	4
Matthew Seegelaar	5
Steven Baylis	6
Claire Snelling	6
Laura Blackhall	7
Eleanor Brown	8
William Kinchin	8
Cyrus Rashvand	9
Olivia Huntley	10
Jenna Ward	11
Elizabeth Tait	12
Lawrence Payne	12
Hayley Mather	13
Rob Way	13
Rebecca Gilbert	14
Rebecca David	14
Russell Mascarenhas	15
Emma Taylor	16
Joanna Parker	17
Lauren Macrae	17
Tamsin Peachey	18
Andrew Dekker	18
Laura Baker	19
Ruth Button	20

Britannia High School

Shema Islam	20
Craig Ingram	21
Gemma Stockton	21
Parminder Singh Mann	22

Adam James Hadley	22
Amiee Johnstone	23
Craig Charles Wardle	24
Shaun Morris	24
Craig Martin	25
Natalie Hart	26
Lee Cox	26
Kelly Graham	27
Shelley Whitehouse	27
Rhona Worth	28
Georgina Westwood	28
Katie Hackett	29
Joanna Lee	30
Joe Hill	30
Emma Southall	31
Mark Blakeway	32

Edgecliff High School

Charlotte Troman	32
Paul Brown	33
Robert Oakes	33
David Tees	34
James Turrell	35
Emma Joshua	36

Fairfax School

Claire Whelan	37
George Francis	37
Tim Brown	38
Caroline Wilson	38
Simon Watts	39
Peter Froggatt	39
Olivia Foster	40
Shaun Willetts	41
Nina Taylor	42
Richard Kiely	42
Tom Long	43
Jenna Hanson	43

Amy Forrest	44
Kayleigh Taylor	44
Adam Winstanley	45
Laura Wale	46
Ciaran Maguire	46
Cara Lawson	47
Elaine Londesborough	48
Liam Ball	48
Josie Hayes	49
Heather Clarke	50
Hannah Johnston	51
Neil Scantlebury	52
Liam Sheena	53
Lucy Coton	54
Nicky Jones	54
Jenny Newman	55
Richard Hathaway	55
Sophie Turner	56
Sammy Kelland	56
Elia Islip	57
Kirsty Jones	58
Anneliese Mountford	58
James Morris	59
Philip Hamilton	59
Nicole Dunn	60
Angelina Rose	61
Louise Matthews	62
Chris Smith	63
Ian Standley	64
Kirsty Cotterill	64
Adam Bennett	65
Mandy Richards	65
Katy Pemberton	66
Laura Green	67
Anne-Marie Tarver	68
Ben Webster	68
Natalie Hull	69
James Simkins	70

Stephanie Tisdale	70
Rupinder Kaur	71
Jamie Ward	71
Gemma Clarke	72
Holly Lewis	73
Luke Renfrew	73
Stephen Gater	74
Dan Wells	75
Simon Gore	76
James Moore	77
Vicky Yau	78

Great Wyrley High School

Victoria Rocks	78
David Mouatt	79
Katie Pawlowski	79
James Wilton	80
Jennifer Smith	81
Emma Foster	82
Natalie Hall	82
Natalie Till	83
Angela Hawkins	84
Peter Harris	84
Victoria Evans	85
Jenna Strange	86
Martin Popov	86
Amanda Pearce	87
Emma Spencer	88
Richard Footman	89
Kerri Baker	90
Christopher Stokes	90
Laura Sensier	91
Emma Strange	92
Sarah Robinson	92
Lindsay Joynes	93
Richard Armstrong	94
Laura Sutton	94
Claire Parfitt	95

Joanne Nicholls	95
Michelle Morgan	96
Amy Finney	96
Claire Ramsdale	97
Stuart Gregory	98
Louise Clare	98
Daniel James Wilson	99
Emma Woodward	99
Sarah Walker	100
Jamie Manson	100
Gemma Botterill	101
Mark Reece	102
Amy Sensier	102
Mark Bartlam	103
Nichola Arrowsmith	104
Gavin Wheatley	104
Lisa-Marie Bowker	105
Sonia Adshead	105
Jenine Fellows	106
Richard Nicholls	106
Lee Goodall	107
Emily Cartwright	108
Krysia Baker	108
Jemma Moran	109
Gemma Biddulph	110
Helen Fleming	110
Charlotte Wood	111
Emily Brown	112
Victoria Dean	113
Andrew Hulme	114
Matthew Fletcher	114
Siobhan Connolly	115
Amy Smith	116
Sarah Lewis	116
Vicky Barrow	117
Zoe Teale	118
Lucia Grennan	118
Lawrence Garbett	119

Katy Owen	119
Lucy Ansell	120
Jenny Hunt	120
Jenny Tibbitts	121
Adam Rolls	122
Tara Bevan	122
Sarah Williams	123
Kirsty Smith	123
Lynne Woodcock	124
Adrian Bullock	124
Leanne Reece	124
Harry Peake	125
Matthew Davis	125
Lisa Carroll	126
Chantelle Benton	126
Matthew Harper	127
Matthew Hibbs	127
Andrew Jennings	128
Tara Pearce	128
Hayley Myles-Blower	129
Gavinder Pawar	129
Jennika Patel	130

Heathfield GM High School

Kelly Thompson	130
Claire Graham	131
Shafeeq Mohammed	131
Jason Jeavons	132
Amy Butler	132
Gemma Glasby	133
Amy Blick	134
Tara Arshad	135
Martyn Barnbrook	135
Michelle York	136
Sean Tobin	136
Stuart Kettle	137
Samina Begum	138
Rebecca Morgan	139

Joseph Leckie School

Andrew Worley	139
Jaswant Gill	140
Brijesh Maisuria	140
Seema Lal	141
Carl Hayes	141
Randip Basra	142
Aarefa Mulla	142
Sophia Azam	143
Amandeep Sambi	144
Zobea Raza	144
Alan Williams	145
Gavin Jukes	146
Gamal Idris	146
Ian Freeth	147
Dipesh Patel	148
Rumi Choudury	148
Tanya Hayes	149
Asma Begum	150
Hema Pandya	151
Kirendeep Attwal	152
Emma McDonald	153
Rumela Begum	154

Saint Martin's School for Girls

Joanna Sidhu	154
Kate Stone	155
Sophie Gibson	155
Rebecca Dudill	156
Amy Walton	156
Joanna McDonagh	157
Ailish Cotter	157
Amy Smith	158
Lucy Archer	158
Kate Pomeroy	159
Christine George	160
Jenny Pallett	160
Victoria Lucas	161

	Samantha Greenfield	161
	Ruth Ainsworth	162
	Ciara Phillips	162
	Lucinda Manning-Brown	163

St Thomas More RC Comprehensive School
	Bhinder Chopra	164

Selly Oak Special School
	Emma Holland	165
	Rebecca Griffin	166
	Anthony Boyce	167
	Michael Edwards	167

Sherbourne Fields School
	Joseph Gilbey	168
	Max Garelick	168
	Emma Barnes	168
	Gagandeep Dogra	169
	John Lawlor	169

Solihull School
	Ian Smith	170
	Yitao Duan	171
	Will Hudson	172
	John Swani	173
	Oliver Manning-Brown	174
	Mark Askew	175
	Richard Howell	176
	Fred Hopkins	176
	Christopher Edwards	177
	James Clarke	178
	David Massey	179
	Richard Bower	180
	Gurinder Sunner	181
	Alex Homer	182
	Tom Osborne	182
	Tom Willshaw	183

Robert Scott	184
Jonathan Thorne	185
Jamie Partington	186

Summerhill School

Adam Lester	187
Sam Robbins	188
Natalie Jones	189
Melissa Doody	190
Kate Hamer	191
Frances Bennett	192
Zoe Riley	193
Karl Oakley	194
Jane Cutler	194
Callum Bradley	195
Danny Thurley	196
Kimberley Hamilton	197
Louise Hickman	198
Mark Hancocks	199
David Owen	200
Sarah Croft	201
Amy Macklin	202
Claire Thomas	203
Danielle Curtis	204
Mary-Kate Thornton	205
Ben Cole	206
Nick Capewell	207
Sarah Foster	208
Emma Osbourn	209
Matthew Wassell	210
Ben Packwood	211

Sutton Coldfield Girls' School

Meloney Rodney	212
Gemma Soden	213
Nyla Yousuf	214
Lydia Corbett	214
Lucy Ray	215

Sehreen Riaz	216
Thu Huong Nguyen	217
Gillian Fildes	218

The High Arcal School

Rupinder Kalsi	219
Laura Rudd	220
Samantha Vanes	220
Vikki Loach	221
Shelley Haldron	221
Jenna Grainger	222
John Humphries	222
Sarah Louise Marsh	223
Michelle Jones	223
Lydia Rodgers	224
Oliver Watchorn	225
Scott Evans	226
Marc Skeldon	226
Helen Harris	227
Wayne Grose	227
Susan Howell	228
Rachel Wildman	228

The Streetly School

Laura Gibbons	229
Naomi Smith	229
Thomas Folan	230
Thomas Cole	230
Luke Crawford	231
Sarah Underwood	232
Richard Bignell	232
William Willis	233
Victoria King	234
Eleanor Jones	235
Chevon Morgan	236
Hayley Aston	237
Christopher Westwood	238
Laura Eadon	238

Danielle Clarke	239
Elize Bevan	239
Joanna Hall	240
Collette Tomkins	240
Aaron Acton	241
Allanah Marsham	242
Katie Gettings	242
Alex Wetton	243
Sarah-Jane Lloyd	244
Kelly Craddock	244
Mark Carmichael	245
Elizabeth Sealey	246
Catherine Patterson	246
Holly Dugmore	247
Adam Whitehead	248
James Kimberley	248
Sally Peel	249
Paul Morris	250
Chantel Reynolds	250
Amritpal Thiara	251
Hannah Motzheim	252
Sophie Nuttall	252
Gemma Alexander	253
Richard Wellings	254
Jade Thomason	254
Judith Buckley	255
Kim Mills	256
Aaron Rhodes	256
Rosalind Jones	257
Gary Bailey	257
Sean Davies	258
David Underwood	258
Rebecca Floyd	259
Sarah Neale	260

Willingsworth High School
Gary Chandler	261
David Evans	262

Stephanie Brookes	262
Paul Powell	263
Hayley Jones	264
Christopher Anslow	264
Sarah Edwards	265
Shaun Burton	266
Rachel Arnold	266
Dean Birch	267
Jonathan Hancock	268
Laura Evans	268
Lee West	269
Tara Houldey	269
Vicky Martin	270
Jane Kirkham	270
Alison Joiner	271
Rebecca Hartshorn	272
Nicholas Slym	273
Craig Ratcliffe	274
Stacey Farmer	274
Aimee Noone	275
Paul Shaw	275
Ross Griffiths	276
Natasha Hickman	276
Thomas Hayward	277
Brian Wright	278
Michelle Howes	278
Nicola Shaw	279
John Flavell	280
Lynsey Arnold	280
Laura Cartwright	281
Tracey McFarlane	282
Beryl Evans	283
Ben Pearce	284
Rachael Jones	284
Lee Kendall	285
Samantha Capewell	286
Paul Holl & Gavin Woodhouse	286
Sarah Edwards & Kay Humphries	287

Stacey Evans	287
Vicki Bentley	288
Matthew Rudge	288
Terri Steventon	289
Sarah Martin	289
Nathan Smart	290
Zoe Patel	290
Samantha Steventon	291
Samantha Richards	292
Stephanie Dicken	293
Jarrad Cole	294
Rebecca Vaughan	294
Leanne Edmunds	295
Tommy Silvester	295
Jonelle Harvey	296
Laura Paskin	297
Jodie Stanford	298
Paul Aston	298
Natasha Collins	299
Stacey Whiles	300
Laura Powell	300
Craig Jones & Adam Rudge	301
Gareth Berrow	302
Shaun Hobday	302
Laura Amy Saunders	303
Amy Hunter	304
Lynseyann Aston	304
Nina Howen	305
Anneka Styles	305
Leighanne Pick	306
Smita Randeria	306
Samantha Bibb	307
Linda Fennell	307
Adam Pullen	308
Zoë Carr	309
Matthew Timms	309
Kaleigh Garratt	310
Samantha Beeston	311

The Poems

The Conker Tree

The horse chestnut leaves blush pink
with their pleasure,
As excited faces forage round for
their treasure.
A white spongy void and used
empty sockets,
The shiny brown eyes seen bulging
in pockets.

Hanging onto the end, the wind
shares them equal,
The first harvest collected, then
tomorrow the sequel.
Such huge potential tossed into a
bag,
Its life ending there it seems really
quite sad.

For those ones discarded and dulling
with time,
It would seem that they shrivel in
shame past their prime,
The future of autumn is in their
robust shell,
They'll grow to share their own
fruitful swell!

Debbie Harrison (18)

WHAT?

Look at him just standing there,
All alone without a care,
Green as grass,
Red as fire,
Growing a bit
Every hour,

Soon it will grow,
As big as a tower,
Look at that,
Little, innocent flower,

Some are big,
Some are small,
Some are short,
Some are tall,

Red ones, blue ones
Yellow ones too,
Any colour,
It's up to you,

Water them,
Feed them,
Basically take care,
And they'll always be right there.

Alison Smith (12)
Arden School

FRIDAY THE 13TH

When I awoke this morning,
The sky was full of rain,
I wondered what the matter was,
Then knew I was in pain,
I had a rotten toothache,
To the dentist I must go,
Where he would drill and fill it,
Oh no! Oh no! Oh no!

I walked towards the bathroom,
To wash and comb my hair,
Then stumbled on my dressing gown,
And fell across a chair,
My glass of milk went flying,
Landing on the floor,
Splattering all the homework
I'd done the night before.

I ran downstairs so quickly,
For I knew that I was late,
To find my mother waiting
With my breakfast on a plate.
I looked up at the calendar
And then it was so plain,
The day that I'd been dreading
Had come around again.

Alix Windsor (12)
Arden School

WINTER POEM

Snow running down your face and red noses too,
Warm woollen mittens and the snow sticks like glue,
Snowmen with carrot noses all grinning with delight,
Children having a snowball fight, be careful not to get frostbite!

Hair turns to icicles, snowballs hit you in your face,
Snowflakes rush from the sky like a giant race,
You look out of the window and all you see is frost,
Children get worried, thinking Santa's got lost.

Water freezes and becomes a cold ice-rink,
The days grow shorter and the sky turns pink,
Christmas trees appear in windows and robins sing in their nests,
Christmas is just simply the best!

Rebecca Thomas (12)
Arden School

THE LONELY TREE

The tree stood in the ground stiff and worn,
Its branches were curled and the leaves torn,
The wind whirled around the tree,
Angry, lashing, dangerously.

The tired tree began to rock instead,
Still the wind chased around its head.
The tree's sharp branches swept the floor,
And its ancient, crooked body bent even more.

The powerful wind, forced and cracked.
First the tree broke and then it snapped.
It lay very still on the ground,
Everything was quiet, not one sound.

Rachel Bromley (13)
Arden School

MY RACE

I am at the gala
waiting for my race
My fear must show
all over my face

My legs are like jelly
I don't feel too good
I hope I do as well
as I think I should

My tummy is all a-quiver
as I put on my goggles
What time I should get
Oh the mind boggles

I'm standing on the blocks
ready to go
The starter says 'Take your marks
ready' *Wow!*

I'm swimming through the water
as fast as I can
I get to the end
and then *Slam!*

I got a good time
Hip hip hooray
I can't wait to tell my mum
I had a good day.

Matthew Seegelaar (12)
Arden School

FOOTBALL

A ball is kicked
A player runs
To catch up with the ball.
Ready to kick
To a team mate or into the goal.

Passed one then another,
Getting closer to the goal.
Tension spreads across the ground.
He draws back his foot,
Shoots hard,
The ball is flying through the air.
The keeper standing petrified,
Motionless
Then with all his power,
Dives towards the post.

He saves the ball,
With all his might.
Team mates congratulate him,
The game goes on.

Steven Baylis (13)
Arden School

THE NEW GIRL IN SCHOOL!

Everything is very big,
And very scary too,
I don't know where the art class is,
And where is the loo?

Getting up in the morning,
Making toast and tea,
Shouting at my sister,
'Help, I've got PE.'

My friends are at the corner,
'Hurry up' they say
'What did you do in drama?'
'Oh we did a play.'

Well the first week's over,
It wasn't really that bad.
I've got a lot of homework,
Who will help me? Dad.

Claire Snelling (11)
Arden School

AUTUMN

The autumn leaves are falling,
Early in the morning,
The mist is covering the ground,
With not so much as a sound,
All the leaves are falling, drifting, floating, wafting,
Falling to the ground.

All the colours of the leaves,
The ones that have fallen from the trees,
Brown, yellow, orange and red,
When all the world's still safe in bed,
All the colours of the leaves,
Brown, yellow, orange and red.

Conkers in their prickly shells,
From the horse chestnut tree they fell,
Squirrels scamper from their drey,
Collecting acorns day by day.
They store their findings safe and sound,
Winter, winter's on its way!

Laura Blackhall (11)
Arden School

THE BUILDING SITE

Big walls are looming over us,
Blocking out the daylight,
Blocking out the fun we once had.
The beauty of this world is slowly
being built upon.
And as I watch, I know why.

Buildings like dark clouds,
thundering over us.
Blocking out the sun,
Casting shadows on the life
we once had.

We loved it,
But now we've covered it with
shining towers of metal.
And it's nearly gone.

Eleanor Brown (13)
Arden School

A NOISY NIGHT

The full moon came out at night
as two cats began to fight
The stars twinkled overhead
while everybody was in bed

They spit, they spat
they screamed and scrawled
Which made the house owners
get up and bawl

Lights came on
the cats got scared
Jumped off the fence
in deep suspense

The cats got up
and ran back home
Then the moon
was left alone.

William Kinchin (11)
Arden School

THE AMBUSH OF HUATL

As the Necromancer marched the living dead to the main battle,
Hails of arrows fell,
They were under attack!
They turned to face the enemy who were the Lizardmen
With their scaly skin and cold blood.

Once the chariot had almost been destroyed via poisoned arrows.
The skeletons charged the Sauras, the big Lizardmen,
When the Necromancer challenged the Champion,
The Necromancer killed him before he could attack,
Though they did get destroyed.
The Zombies held on against the smaller Skinks.

The Mummies charged the Saurus
Making them flee and get destroyed,
The Mummies then charged the other unit of Skinks,
Also making them get destroyed via fleeing,
The archer on the destroyed chariot
Shot the Skink general dead,
But the Skinks stood still to make it a draw.

Cyrus Rashvand (12)
Arden School

AUTUMN'S MARK

It is autumn,
The leaves have lost their vibrant yellow,
they are beginning to turn red
Ready to retreat
to a heap of compost.

The wind is like ice,
Whipping around us like an
endless whirlpool.
As dawn breaks,
the larks begin to sing.

The frost is beginning
to leave the silver
glittering mark of winter.

The sky is grey and
unwelcoming,
far away I can hear the
distant waves
crashing against the merciless
rocks.

Olivia Huntley (11)
Arden School

The News

Posted through the letterbox in an
official brown envelope
Marked with 'OHMS Hand-deliver to the
door',
Dreaded was the letter he received on
that dull morning,
Hated for its message 'You are required
at war'

He had feared that letter since the day
he'd got back from Japan,
All his awful memories had begun to
disappear,
Now a man of 36 he thought his
soldier's days were over
But now he had to face it all and go
off to Korea

The day he went he left behind his
loving wife and sons
With no idea if or when he ever would
return
The news had completely torn apart an
innocent family's lives,
Our world is obsessed by power
When will we ever learn?

Jenna Ward (13)
Arden School

THE HUNTER AND THE HUNTED

She stands firm and tall,
Her grand grey body blocking out the sun,
She looks to her child oblivious of
The next moment.

Beyond the lake,
In the forest of reeds,
Stands a man and a gun,
He smiles meanly,
Seeing only the money for her blood,
He moves closer, closer

Ready for the kill,
Bang! The elephant falls to the ground,
With a crash that rocks the earth,
He picks out her tusks,
The only thought of money,
The mean hunters and the innocent hunted.

Elizabeth Tait (14)
Arden School

SNOWBOARDING

A feeling of adrenalin,
When rushing down the hills,
The pines and snow-capped mountains
Are a backdrop for my thrills.

On my snowboard, on my own,
I go skimming down the slopes,
To the sound of gushing wind
And the heartbeat of my hopes.

Lawrence Payne (11)
Arden School

The Sea

My castle standing still and untouched,
but see across the shining sand,
that enemy called the sea creeps slowly to my castle walls,
advancing stealthily.
My favourite castle far on edge standing by the sea,
the wave might creep up to it maybe even me.
The sun glistened in the distance watching over me,
Whilst I forget about sandcastles and think about the sea.
I think about the creatures far beneath the sea,
swimming all about the place looking up at me.
I think about the flower-bed way down there, bright colours
delicate petals and the sparkle of them everywhere.
Above the sea my sandcastle stands in a pile of ruins,
my work is all undone,
I work again watching the sea
creeping up to my sandcastle maybe even me.

Hayley Mather (12)
Arden School

Night-Time Fears

When I go to bed at night my mum says goodnight.
Then she goes out and switches off the light.
All those shadows on the wall
Could be demons come to call.
My hamster spinning in his wheel so late
Sounds like a creaky, squeaky old gate,
Then the footsteps on the stairs, this could be really bad
Oh! What a relief, it's only Dad.

Rob Way (12)
Arden School

FIRE, FIRE!

The tall, red-hot flames
filled my dry throat choking me.
I crawled around on the
black, charred floor, gasping for fresh, clean air
'I've found it, I've found it' I shrieked.
I stretched out as far as I could to reach for it.
I tried, but I found it too hard.
Something was stopping me.
'I can reach it, I can,' I reminded myself hopefully.
But I couldn't reach it,
although I desperately wanted it,
So I gave up because I was too tired and weak.
I fell to the ground and fell fast asleep.
Where I belonged.

Rebecca Gilbert (13)
Arden School

A POEM FOR MY FAREWELL FRIEND

The two bright white doves fly high in the
blue sky,
They are together but individually fly,
One dove must stay,
One dove must go,
God knows they will meet again and say
'Hello.'
The two bright white doves leave each other's
presence,
But lingering in the air is the remaining
essence,
They will miss each other but will hopefully
find another.

Rebecca David (14)
Arden School

THE DESTRUCTION OF THE STORM

The wind lashed on the window-panes,
The shutters rattled like rusty chains.
The thunder rumbled through the hills,
Its thunderous echoes instilled chills.

The rain whipped through the gloomy wood,
Onward and onward as fast as it could.
The lightning smashed against the ground,
The air was filled with crashing sound.

The sky was ripped open by a blaze of light,
Shattering the darkness of the night.
The thunder boomed like a distant drum,
Sending a message of worse to come.

Against the wind the trees bent double,
Fences were battered until rubble.
Roof tiles, hurled like lethal weapons,
Descended like hailstones from the heavens.

The rain continued unrelenting,
Through the storm its anger venting.
Swollen rivers turned into raging torrents,
Drowning all in swirling currents.

The thunder crashed, the storm grew stronger,
The night dragged on, longer and longer.
The darkness engulfed like a huge black sheet,
Not a soul was to be seen, out in the street.

Suddenly the sky grew calm and light,
The storm had passed right out of sight.
A trail of destruction left in its wake,
How long will recovery take?

Russell Mascarenhas (13)
Arden School

SUICIDE

Walking home,
Feeling down,
Head spinning round and round,
Open the door,
Slam it shut,
Run upstairs to cry and cry
Open the diary,
Enter in today's events
Fell out with Kate,
Rowed with Mum,
Had a detention
With Mr Black,
Bullied by the 'A' gang yet again
Phone rang,
It's Kate's new friend
Calling me all the names under the sun
Slam down the phone and cry some more,
Take my coat and leave a note,
Grab a bus, pay the fare,
Say a prayer,
Walk down to the water's edge
Say goodbye
Then . . .

Emma Taylor (14)
Arden School

THANK YOU FOR BEING MY FRIEND

When I needed you
You were there.
When I was hurt,
You eased the pain.
When I was angry,
You calmed me down.
What would I do without you?

You are my special friend,
I could trust you with my life,
I would do anything for you,
Many things I could not have done without you.
I am forever thankful.

Joanna Parker (13)
Arden School

THE PHOTOGRAPH

I look at a photograph what do I see?
The image of who I used to be.
The long plait and a big smile
She and I haven't met for a while.

When I think about what has changed
I feel laughter, death and pain
But I'm sure the same girl is still inside
Who is kind and shy and has nothing to hide.

In ten years' time what will my photograph show?
Will I look different? What will I know?
No one knows what the future will hold,
But the girl in the photograph is going to be bold.

Lauren Macrae (14)
Arden School

DEVIL'S HUNT

She looks, she stares, sniffs the air,
And goes without another care,
A smell of sweetness in the atmosphere,
Shattered by the danger near,
With tail flicking,
And whiskers twitching,
Her eyes take on a glassy depth,
For she can hear the devil's breath,

Perhaps today she will die,
I know it won't be dignified.

Tamsin Peachey (14)
Arden School

TOOTHPASTE

Wibbly, wobbly
Squibbly, squabbly
Bibbly, bobbly toothpaste

It squidges out of the tube
Like a squidgy, wiggly worm
How do those colours stay straight?
Why don't those colours mix?
Those colours always fix

Isn't it annoying when that silly tube does split
All over your hands and all over your shirt
Why is it so messy?

Andrew Dekker (12)
Arden School

I Wonder?

The deep church bell cries out each hour
While children happily play,
Their parents are earning money,
For a family every day.

But parents are all different,
Their tastes just don't agree,
Why is the world changing,
Or is that just me?

I don't know why this happens,
It's just my mind I think,
Sometimes I really wonder,
If we could have that link.

Can't we all be kind?
It's not that hard to do,
If only you had a heart,
You would understand me too.

Laura Baker (13)
Arden School

WHALES, A CLOSE ENCOUNTER

Swimming, gliding so gracefully through the water,
Silently echoing your sweet melodies of enchanting music,
I wonder, do you know your friends are being killed?
Sacrificed for the greediness of man.

Rising and falling with the waves, going forwards never look back,
Unaware they may strike you next,
You look so beautiful, at peace with the ocean,
The sparkling turquoise water glistens upon your back.

You gently surface and let out a silent fountain of raindrops,
Your eyes burn deep into mine,
You've engraved your name upon my heart,
I'm not letting you go.

Ruth Button (13)
Arden School

WITCHES, ZOMBIES AND GHOSTS

Witches do have nasty habits.
They eat bats, snails and rabbits,
When they see the full moon.
They stir their potion with a spoon.
The ghosts just wander about,
The little children scream and shout,
That night wasn't a pretty sight.
I think it was the worst night,
When the children are asleep in their rooms,
The witches fly up with their brooms.
While the witches stir their cauldrons
The ghosts grab little children.

Shema Islam (11)
Britannia High School

BUBBLE TROUBLE

The cauldron creaks upon the floor
Waiting to be used once more.
In goes the water
With a splutter
And a dead toad from the gutter.

Bubble, bubble lots of trouble
Bubble, bubble lots of trouble

Creak, creak, creak
In goes a sheep
Hey you, don't have a peek.

Bubble, bubble lots of trouble
Bubble, bubble lots of trouble

This shall make you disappear
And you shall never reappear.

Craig Ingram (11)
Britannia High School

SPELLBOUND

*S*pooky, slimy, horrible and scared
*P*ulling and tugging my jumper teared
*E*ventually I got free
*L*eave me, leave me I can't see
*L*oosen me, loosen me I want to be free
*B*ump, I fell on the floor
*O*ut I go I headed straight for the door
*U*nder the tables over the chairs everywhere it was there
*N*early there Oh but it wasn't fair
*D*angerous, deadly, deceiving dare.

Gemma Stockton (13)
Britannia High School

SPELLBOUND

Boil, boil, boil my trouble!
Wham, bam, alakazam!
When it is midnight on my broomstick.
I shall send a fright.
If anyone tries to stop me, I shall get my husband; the wizard
He'll turn them into an ugly lizard.
Then they'll be frightened of the wizard and me.
Like a cat they'll go scampering up a tree.

Put in some branches from a tree
And to be nasty I'll throw in some frog's wee!
Put in some toenails
Oh yes! Some dirty slimy snails.
It'll crackle, it'll crackle whilst it's being done.
This spell will be done in the time
When Big Ben will chime
Hocus pocus!
Nocus locus! This spell is nearly done
When the world's mine they'll be working for me.
Controlling them, boy that'll be fun.

Parminder Singh Mann (11)
Britannia High School

SPELLBOUND

Witches are true
Making spells all through the night
Destroying all they see
So watch out at Hallowe'en
Because they'll come
And try a spell.

Adam James Hadley (11)
Britannia High School

SPELLBOUND

*S*pit, spat, titter, tatter, spit, spat
*P*itter-patter on the window-pane
*E*lizabeth my dear, come down, stop looking at the rain.
*L*isa, Lee yes everyone tonight shall dress up from head to toe.
*L*et me go, let me go, please Mum let me go.
*B*oo the children will let out, trick or treat they will shout.
*O*liver and Oscar are going too, Mum please let me go,
                                  guess who's going 'you'
*U*p and down and around we'll go singing, laughing
                                  telling jokes, it's not fair.
*N*icola please tell Mum, it's not fair
*D*own dark streets we'll go, that'll give you a scare.

*S*abrina, what Mum, shouldn't sisters stick together?
*P*lease Mum let me go, pick me up from Emma's, I'll ask Emma.
*E*mma said she'll go round with me
*L*et her go Mum, she won't get in trouble just you see
*L*isa's going, are you sure?
*B*ound to be, I'll ask, she's just next door.
*O*ver the fence my sister went, come back with news to tell,
                                  she'll tell you in a minute.
*U*nder the door came a scraggy note and on it she wrote,
                                  yes, I can go, can you?
*N*otes flew round until half past two.
*D*own to Emma's we did go, to trick or treat with
                                  Emma, George, Lee and Joe.

Amiee Johnstone (13)
Britannia High School

THE SPELL!

Cats' tails and frogs' brains
And, urine dripping down the drains
Witch's arm and human's bladder
Toads and frogs and my next door's
Poisonous adder.

All that goes into my pot
I like this spell quite a lot
Newts' eyes and lizards' intestines
And hearts from Frankensteins.

Witches' warts and a fingernail
And cow's udder that is pale
A man's spirit and a dog's leg
And a chicken's rotten egg.

Tiger's liver and dragons' hearts
And some ugly bat parts
Owl beaks that go coo.

At last my spell is done
I thought that was fun
I will get myself a brew
To get ready for my stew.

Craig Charles Wardle (11)
Britannia High School

BOIL THE WATER WITH...

The cauldron pot
On the fire warming up
And in the cauldron were toads
Dead toads, cats and all the other things in the witch's cauldron.

*C*auldron pot
*A*lways hot
*T*oads in it everywhere
*S*o are all animals.

Shaun Morris (11)
Britannia High School

SPELLBOUND!

A dash of potion,
A dragon's liver,
Some slimy snakes that slide and slither,
Creepy crawlies,
Phantom's blood,
Some gooey ectoplasm that looks like mud.

Vampire venom,
Skeleton bones,
Something that creaks, moans and groans,
Newts' eyes.
Frogs' toes,
Some man-eating plants that grow, grow, grow.

Potions,
Zombies,
Wizard's spells
Big brown bats,
A cauldron boils.

Puff, bang, crash and whizz
A cackle from a wicked witch
Hocus pocus, toil and trouble
Go away or you're in trouble!

Craig Martin (11)
Britannia High School

THE WITCH'S BROTH

In the frog's legs go,
Then the pond water cold as snow,
Circles, squares any shape you like,
Put them in to give someone a *Fright!*

Double, trouble burn and bubble,
Frogs will burn but crabs will cause trouble.

Next the spiders will flow,
So the mice will not go.
Now you put pens and pencils,
In the broth, with other utensils.

Double, trouble, burn and bubble,
Spiders will burn, but cats will cause trouble.

When you put everything in,
You will be poisoned and this will be sin!

Natalie Hart (11)
Britannia High School

SPELLBOUND

*S*pooky spooks up the stairs
*P*eople screaming everywhere
*E*verlasting sounds up in the air
*L*eave some bread out every night
*L*ibily boo the night goes through
*B*roomsticks flying up in the air
*O*ogie boogies in my room
*U*nder my bed I hear strange sounds
*N*early all the men are gonks on Hallowe'en
*D*ear oh dear I've got to wait till next year.

Lee Cox (12)
Britannia High School

SPELLBOUND

A spell can be scary full of wizardry and fun,
There are spells that will leave you
sad and miserable when done,
A spell can be magic or maybe not,
A spell can be made in a cauldron or pot,
Spells can be made of evil and deceit,
Or spells can be made from old smelly feet,
You can be caught in a spell of love,
Or maybe of money,
But be warned it may backfire and
you'll be turned into a bunny.
I've given you a warning so reader
beware, if you're going to do magic
stop and think you might get a scare!

Kelly Graham (13)
Britannia High School

SPELLBOUND

A spell is a spell, a witch is a witch,
if you bug me I'll give you a twitch.
A spell is a spell, a wizard is a wizard
Go away or I'll trap you in a blizzard.
A spell is a spell, a cat is a cat,
Jump up and down or I'll turn you into a bat.
A spell is a spell, a hog is a hog,
come near me and you'll be a frog.
A spell is a spell, a friend
is a friend and this is
where my poem ends.

Shelley Whitehouse (13)
Britannia High School

SPELLBOUND

I went to bed late one night
Switched off my bedroom light
The cat jumped up onto my bed
Hang on! The cat is dead!
My bedroom mat came alive
And did a funky little jive
My curtains started walking
And talking to my switch!
Then suddenly appeared a witch
In a horrid green mist.
'Hello Rhona' she evily hissed.
'We need to hold a monster mash
But we are short of cash'
I really thought I was gonna die
So with a sigh
I said 'Hold it here'
Witches, vampires, werewolves and monsters come around
While I joined in, totally *Spellbound!*

Rhona Worth (13)
Britannia High School

SPELLBOUND

On one misty Hallowe'en night,
Something gave me quite a fright.
To find out what it was that scared me,
Listen now, very carefully.

Vampires, witches, spiders, ghosts,
A strange man who opened up his huge coat,
And out came a flock of bats,
Who seemed to be devising with the witches' black cats.

Mystical pumpkins and spooky skeletons,
Serial killers with knives for weapons.
Wizards putting people into a trance,
And people chanting as they dance.

Gruesome, grotesque and eerie monsters,
All with slimy and squidgy furs.
The werewolf's howl ended the night,
The night that gave me quite a fright.

Georgina Westwood (11)
Britannia High School

SPELLBOUND

It's not just yet but coming soon,
It's the night with a full moon,
All the graves are opened up,
The ghosts came out walking on bare foot,
They stare at you right in your face,
They haunt you *Boo!* In any place,
Vampires, zombies, mummies too,
They're out there and they're haunting you.
Some people say that ghosts aren't real,
You won't say that if you're their meal,
Witches, wizards and black cats,
Most of the witches wear black hats,
Remember a witch always has a spell,
She'll probably throw you down a well,
In a haunted house you hear a scream,

Watch out 'cause it's Hallowe'en!

Katie Hackett (11)
Britannia High School

SPELLBOUND

One night there was
a ghost and witches
all about and it was
scary and horrible.
There were bats and ghosts
and skeletons all over
the place and the witches
made all kinds of things
like poisons, disappearing
tricks and magic.
And they all scared me
The cats were all over the place and
they were ugly and disgusting
And there were old bats all of them.
They were scary.

Joanna Lee (11)
Britannia High School

SPELLBOUND

Have you ever heard about.
The headless lady shopper?
She shops at any shopping store.
She really is a shocker.

She scares off all the people.
Who are shopping all today.
The headless lady comes every month,
Including March and May.

First! She looks normal.
Looks absolutely right.
But then she pulls her head right off.
It really is a fright.

But all she does when she scares.
Is make a screaming noise.
She always shoots the ladies and girls.
But rips open all the guys.

So beware out there!

Joe Hill (11)
Britannia High School

SPELLBOUND

Is it realistic or is it fake,
Is it round the corner or straight
through the garden gate,
A witch on a broomstick it's magic, scary
but it's true,
Or could it be a ghost in a graveyard,
and it's after you.
Spooky vampires in the dark, drinking
people's blood.

The moon is full it's time to take your bed
and go to sleep.
In the night you hear strange noises
it's dark and you are scared.
Which one is it, I don't know just you stay
prepared!

Emma Southall (11)
Britannia High School

SPELLBOUND

S o you think you're not scared
P retending to be brave
E vil is for zombies laying in their grave
L eeches sucking your blood
L abyrinths where you lose your soul
B ound to scare you
O ut of your hood
U nder a spell
N ewt's eye, mouth and tail
D ead things just want to make you wail.

Mark Blakeway (11)
Britannia High School

ONE GLOOMY MORNING

One gloomy morning, when the stars were still up high,
I saw the planet Jupiter, way up in the sky,
I saw a man up in the sky, his beard so dark and grey,
Mars, Saturn, Pluto and then the Milky Way.

Then one dark and silent night, when mom was still asleep,
I heard knocking on my window so I went over for a peep,
The screams and shouts around my mind, and what a funny sound,
Screams and shouts about my room and howling of a hound.

The nightmare of a dragon, who fires in the night,
No dreams are allowed here only nightmares that will fright,
The terror of a witch, that will turn you to a frog,
And the growling of a werewolf that used to be a dog.

Charlotte Troman (12)
Edgecliff High School

WHY WE FELL OUT

We fell out I don't know why
Late that night you made me cry
We fell out because of the milkman
I wouldn't have tried it on with another woman
You said he was really great
How I found you, must have been fate
In the bedroom on the floor
That's why I kicked him out the door
Sometimes clever people can work things out
But I think I'd rather shout
Now you're gone, I've told Uncle Terry
Before we split up I was seeing his secretary.

Paul Brown (15)
Edgecliff High School

THE BOMB

I heard the whirring blades of B-29s.
Then that awful sound of the siren going off.
A flash of light followed that.
A shower of buildings showered on people.
A great immense heat spread upon the burning landscape.
I got out of the shelter and looked around.
Flies were landing on the exposed flesh of naked bodies.
People halfway through windows, struggling to escape,
But never making it.
Black rain poisoned with radiation fell on the
innocent victims and on the land.
People dead and dying from the devastation of one weapon,
The *Nuclear bomb*.
Why?
Why us?

Robert Oakes (13)
Edgecliff High School

THE BOMB

A plane in the sky,
Everyone running for cover,
That ear-splitting noise of the siren.
And then *silence*.
Everyone hiding waiting for the blast,
Waiting for the end,
Then it comes, the noiseless flash.
Then comes the screams of the people,
People trapped in cellars,
And people trapped under broken beams,
People dying.
Millions of dead lying in the road.
A great big hole where the city used to be.
And here comes the black rain,
To kill all who try to survive.
To die a long agonising death.
Why us?
Why them?
Why anyone?
Why?

David Tees (13)
Edgecliff High School

THE BOMB

The B-29 diminished,
A noiseless flash,
A warm explosion,
A flash of blue and white,
The nuclear fireball,
The mushroom cloud,
The powdered abode,
The burning streets,
The darkened sky,
Frantic shrieks,
Critically injured,
Direct burns,
Skin, charcoal black,
The black rain falling,
Polluting the water,
No water
No food
No life
Just radiation
This is the
Power of the
Nuclear bomb.

James Turrell (13)
Edgecliff High School

THE DAY THE WORLD ENDED

From the moment I'm released
I know what I will do, total destruction
I'm going to kill.
As I fall through the air
getting closer to land, the time becomes nearer for the world to soon end!
As I fall on the land
A silent white light gives off radiation to the
people in sight.
Now I have landed, the disasters begin.
Destruction and fire
the town is alight,
the people are screaming to save all their lives,
the wind is horrendous
a mushroom of smoke
the buildings are burning, everyone is hurting
the contaminated water, the food is all gone.
All the burnt bodies just lying alight.
Everybody's searching, searching for help, nobody's
there, there's no one around, they walk in
rubble dead bodies lie burnt
this terrible blast that I have caused has spread all around with a 60m diameter fireball sweeping the ground now everybody's dead all over the world!

Emma Joshua (13)
Edgecliff High School

FRIENDS

Friends are those who are always
there for you.
Listen to you, stick up for you
Friends should give you strong
advice,
And be there in terrible situations.

To be a good friend you should
be caring and kind.
Giving back what a friend
gives to you.

Having a laugh
Crying on their shoulder
Telling you 'That dress really
doesn't suit you.'
Thank God for friends.

Claire Whelan (13)
Fairfax School

FISHES FISH

Fishes fishes swim in the sea,
Why do fishes swim in the sea?
Is it the colour?
Is it the look?
Why do fishes swim in the sea?
What is there to do?
All they seem to do
Is swim about a stick of glue.
It has always puzzled me
Why fishes swim in the sea.

George Francis (13)
Fairfax School

SPACE

Space, what is space?
Is it a never ending darkness
Or is it just an eternity of stars.

Space, what is space?
Is it a mass of unknown planets
Or just a vast clump of meteors.

Space, what is space?
Is it an infinity of universes
Or just a place that people wonder about.

Space, what is space?
Is it a place that waits for what it waits for best?
Nobody knows.

Space, what is space?

Tim Brown (14)
Fairfax School

LIFE

Why does life have such an effect on people,
Why is it so amazing,
Why is it so good and makes people feel full about themselves,
It can be unfair,
Suicidal and cruel
Yet life is not totally miserable all the time
Also not always happy and great.
But remember these words for as long as you like . . .

A life lived in fear is a life half-lived!

Caroline Wilson (12)
Fairfax School

A POEM ON TROLLS

It was a dark and dreary night,
and the wind was howling hard,
everyone had gone to sleep,
so the trolls came out of hiding.
Their ugly little faces,
and their awful rough skin,
make them look so ugly,
they'd make you shiver deep within.

As they came out of the caves in their hundreds,
the trumpets started to sound,
and the army of trolls headed for the town.

They burnt down all the houses,
and the screams were piercingly loud,
they killed most of the people in many miles around.

Suddenly the sun came up,
and the village was left in wrecks,
but the trolls all turned to stone,
or withered like a crisp.

Simon Watts (11)
Fairfax School

WAITING

I wait for you,
For you I wait,
Through the darkest hour of late,
I wait for the day,
For you to say,
You'll come and stay for a day.

Peter Froggatt (13)
Fairfax School

MIDNIGHT IN THE BEDROOM

The days are short the nights long deep in the heart of winter
I wake up shivering
It's like an igloo

My bedroom is pitch black
I can't see anything
All I hear is the dog next door.

Suddenly the dog stops
The clock in the hall strikes twelve
It is the witching hour

I try to turn
Paralysed by fear
As it tingles down my spine.

Frozen to the spot
I see my curtain flying and the window open
I hear a tappety-tap

I go to investigate
Catching my curtain, closing my window
But there is still that tappety-tap

Seeing the moon glowing full in the night sky
It has red eyes they get bigger and bigger
It's impossible, but it is twelve o'clock.

I scream nothing but a squeak
I hear a noise
The moon is speaking

I cannot understand it
It's gobbledegook
The tapping stops the moon disappears.

I am back in my bed with a question to ask
Is there a man on the moon? Or was it a dream?
Maybe it's someone from Apollo Thirteen.

Olivia Foster (12)
Fairfax School

GOLDEN TEAR

The pressure's building,
the riders mount,
the horn goes loud,
I hear the sound,
they're off, they're round,
the first jumps nearly coming up,
leap! One down,
others flying round
12 seconds gone,
the tension's high,
the second jump,
they'll have to fly,
2 more down,
9 still up,
the track bends round,
which horse has won,
the line is near,
it has been such a run,
could it be that one,
or this one here,
we have a winner,
it's Golden Tear.

Shaun Willetts (11)
Fairfax School

THE SIGNS OF AUTUMN

I can always tell when autumn's on its way
The leaves changing from green
To orange,
Burgundy
And yellow
The mornings are duller
The evenings are darker
It gets colder and colder
Wetter and wetter.
All the birds are flying south
For the coming cold weather
Yes,
I can always tell when autumn's on its way.

Nina Taylor (12)
Fairfax School

THE STAR

I am gleaming, I'm a star
watching all from afar.
Looking at the world go by,
sitting in the night sky.
Looking at the moon and stars,
and watching all the moving cars.

Children staring up at me,
my light shining on a tree.
Time to go to their beds,
time to rest their sleepy heads.
Now it's time we've had our fun,
here it comes the bright, bright sun.

Richard Kiely (11)
Fairfax School

MIDNIGHT IN THE DARKNESS

In the dead silence of the night.
The terrors come creeping, moaning, howling.
The sound of the dead

Silenced like a reaper they slowly glide.
All the creatures of the underworld fly tonight.

The smell of rotting flesh and the darkness overwhelming.
Consuming and intimidating in its very own way.

As the pitch black takes over.
Sweeping, soaring, capturing anything in its way.

In the dead silence of the night.
The terrors come creeping, moaning, howling.
The sound of the dead.

Tom Long (12)
Fairfax School

WATER

Water is everywhere,
It's around our feet
Around our body
It's even around
The world.
Water is the sea
Water is our drink
Water is the rain
That soaks us through.

Jenna Hanson (11)
Fairfax School

MIDNIGHT IN THE OLD CHURCH

Walking down a street at midnight,
Enter a very old church,
Stop, look around,
I don't know what to do.

All alone, scared,
Stand as stiff as a statue,
Look around, all I see are spiders' webs,
Blowing in the wind,
Turn to see where the wind is coming from.

The window is smashed,
My hair stands on end,
A shiver goes down my spine,
There becomes a black mist,
I jump out of my skin.

Amy Forrest (12)
Fairfax School

MY FIRST DAY AT INFANTS

Nervous and frightened, yes I was,
The day had just began,
As I started, I was frightened, yes frightened,
Mummy, Mummy please don't leave me,
As she left me I started to cry,
With tears in my eyes I said 'Bye, bye,'
As I stopped crying I could finally see,
A smiling new teacher looking down on me,
My first day at infants was not so bad,
When the day was over I think I was glad!

Kayleigh Taylor (12)
Fairfax School

CYCLING IN THE TOUR DE FRANCE

Cycling is fun all the time,
You'll stop fit and healthy,
Cycling can earn you a lot of money,
Lying down in bed after a stage in the tour,
In the flesh you will be totally and utterly shattered,
Night and day you'll be thinking what went wrong,
Going into the next day you'll be feeling the pain.

In the hotel at night,
Never again! You'll be thinking,

The days you will enjoy on your bike,
His nerves of steel kept him going,
Every day it got worse and worse,

Tour de France he thought why, why, why?
Over and over again he went away,
Under the covers he went at night,
Racing off again and again,

During the day it got hotter and hotter,
Every day it did this,

French fans cheering you on,
Racing, racing, racing faster,
At the finish you can't wait to get off your bike,
Never again he repeats in his sleep,
Cycling is so much fun he says,
Every day he did this in his dreams.

Adam Winstanley (13)
Fairfax School

NIGHT-LIFE

These vile horrible creatures that fly,
Oh so high,
Under the spooky moonlit world.

Not on brooms,
But on their dirty vacuums,
They can cast a spell in a second.

You will have to dodge their magic,
It's more useful than a washing-up gadget,
With their wands.

They also have warts,
The size of tennis courts,
So watch out!

These vile horrible creatures that fly,
Oh so high,
Under the spooky moonlit world,
Still need their bedtime.

Laura Wale (11)
Fairfax School

HALLOWE'EN

It was October the thirty-first,
The night was cold and black,
There were children running around,
All carrying big black sacks.

The boys all dressed as wizards,
Long hats and rubber bats,
The girls all dressed as witches,
Long skirts and big black hats.

They knocked on doors,
And shouted 'Trick or treat,'
The people gave them money,
Or gave them something to eat.

If you asked for a trick,
You'd get a surprise,
It might be nasty,
So it wouldn't be wise.

Ciaran Maguire (12)
Fairfax School

SPELLBOUND

Cobwebs sparkle and shimmer from the beam
of the pumpkin's head.

Ghosts wander about the graveyard to see
the real dead.

Children go to trick of treat for Hallowe'en is here,

Not knowing that the evil is very very near

Where wolves tackle a wizard

While a bony skeleton starts up a blizzard.

A flap of a bat, a leg of a frog, the smell of a mat
all go into the goblin's daunting
spell to lure a child to its sudden doom.

Witches zoom swiftly up into the lighted
moon.

Cara Lawson (11)
Fairfax School

UNTIL

How long will it take?
How many smiles must she make?
Until he notices her

How many years must go by?
Should she sit and cry?
Until he notices her.

How much must she stare
At his golden blond hair?
Until he notices her.

How much must her life be changed?
Everything rearranged
Until he notices her.

Will she have to die?
Jump off a cliff? Try to fly?
Until he notices her.

Or should she ask him out?
Blow it all, no doubt
And then, he will notice her.

Elaine Londesborough (13)
Fairfax School

NATURE

The sun rises
early in the morning
The birds wake
and sing their merry songs.

The bees are busy
collecting pollen
Butterflies are fluttering
along the hedgerows.

The sunset is showing
now the sun has gone down
The birds are quiet
mustn't make a sound.

The bees are home
with their young
The butterflies have gone
back to their home.

Liam Ball (11)
Fairfax School

A DAY IN THE LIFE OF A WITCH

A dingy, dark, creepy house
Home to the sinister witch.
Her only companion, innocent looking
 ever miaowing . . .
The black cat.
Wearing a tall, pointed
 hat
Her long cloak sweeps along
 the floor,
Until her journey - her broomstick
 flight
Takes her into the darkness
 of the night sky.
Soaring, dipping, climbing looping
Cackling, shrieking, hissing, chanting.
When morning breaks,
She returns,
And fills her rusty cauldron
 with her found ingredients . . .
A deadly potion!

Josie Hayes (12)
Fairfax School

WHEN I AM OLD

When I am old I'd like to be,
Kind and generous, happy and free.
With my head in the clouds,
But my feet on the ground.
I don't want to live in a home,
I want to be noble and proud.

I'd like to be slim, tall and fine,
With long flowing hair,
That's radiant with shine.
I'd like to go out, not stay in and shout.
I'd hit the town, go to parties,
Get down!

I'd like to play sports,
Football, hockey, netball, all sorts.
I'd like to have children, with grandkids galore,
I'd spoil them rotten, and totally adore,
Their cute little noses and cute little feet,
I'd be silent and listen,
To their little hearts beat.

Overall when I'm old I'd like to be happy,
I'd spoil their kids, and change their nappy.
I'd like to live to the grand age of ninety,
Now that's all I'll say, so see you,
Good nighty!

Heather Clarke (13)
Fairfax School

LONELINESS

I sit and count the hours,
Waiting for the phone to ring,
Hoping you will be on the other end,
What joy your voice would bring.

I wander through the streets,
Hoping to see you,
How many weeks since we last met?
It must have been a few.

When I get up in the morning,
I look through all the post,
I never hear from you anymore,
You used to write the most.

In the end I ring my Mum,
And ask, 'What's going on?'
But all she says to me is,
'Hannah, your friend has gone.'

It is then I realise,
Why you are ignoring me,
For you have gone away,
And your spirit's been set free.

You went up to heaven last month,
Although I didn't know,
But there is one message for you to remember,
I do love you so.

Hannah Johnston (13)
Fairfax School

A Poem On School

The best years of your life
or so they say,
Is sitting in class
reading and writing all day.
You must behave
you must concentrate,
or else you'll have to
stay behind late.

English, maths, and history
are all supposed
to interest me.
Why can't it just be
games or art,
they are lessons that make you smart.

Dinner times are
usually fun,
playing footy in the sun.

Afternoons go pretty quick
but then there's homework
which makes me sick.

Still only another three years to go
then it's off to work
to earn some dough.

Neil Scantlebury (13)
Fairfax School

ALONE BY MYSELF

When I'm alone at night,
Waiting for a friend to call.
I often give myself a fright,
And think there's someone at the door.
But no not a person as we know.
But a witch or a ghost
That's knocking at my door.
Witches and ghosts,
That lurk behind doors.
Should not be trusted,
For your own cause.

When I'm alone at night watching the TV by myself,
I often wonder about my health.
When I hear a creaking sound,
I turn around and scream and shout.
When I realise it's nothing more,
Than an old tree branch rapping at my door.
Then I see a sinister black cloak,
And a snow-white scary ghost.
Then I realise that I'm not alone.
But a witch and ghost are in my home.

When they finally come to greet me,
I shrivel down and say 'Don't beat me!'
The ghost whined and the witch cackled,
And her potion sizzled and crackled.
They then bent down and stared at me,
I said *'Aaaaaaaagggggggghhhhhhhh!'*
They said *'BBBBUUUURRRRPPPP!'*

Liam Sheena (14)
Fairfax School

SPELLBOUND

Whoosh, going higher and higher in the air, come on keep going
we are almost there,
That was the witches on Hallowe'en night getting ready to
make a big fright.
Toffee apples, candy sweets, that's what the children wanted
to eat,
The witches spied all night waiting to make a big fright,
They got their spell books out one by one looking for the right one.
Slugs' legs and bats' wings, jumping frogs and stinky things,
Cat's tail and spider's web,
They are the ones that will scare off the dead,
They mixed them up by having lots of jolly fun,
They got closer and closer I can't watch what will they do?
Could it be true, is there a witch inside me and you,
Oh no, it went blank my camcorder switched out,
You will have to work the last bit out.

Lucy Coton (11)
Fairfax School

SEA

A sea of blue
A sea of green
Sometimes rough
Sometimes serene
The sea goes in
The sea goes out
Children run and play about
Loads of waves
Splashing through caves
At the end of the day children go home
And the sun sets over the sea.

Nicky Jones (11)
Fairfax School

THE DEADLY MIX IN THE CAULDRON

Boiling bubbling in it goes,
Four fat frogs' legs and five ugly toes.
Two big snails and one whole rat.

Boiling bubbling in it goes,
Ten large lizards and two black cats.
Fourteen toenails with dirt intact.

Boiling bubbling in it goes,
Three drops of ear-wax along with six
eyeballs with a nose or two and a few
eagles' claws.

Stir it, stir it, stir it well, this disgusting
mixture comes from hell.

> So if you drink it please beware
> you might be in for a dreadful scare.

Jenny Newman (12)
Fairfax School

DEATH!

When you die, people say you go to places
Don't know where but I've got a good idea
I imagine a place all white and fluffy
Or to the other extreme, all red and fiery.
In the first account good people go
And the other bad people go
God is in one, and the devil in the other.
God has a good and pleasant world
The devil has a bad and frightening world.

Richard Hathaway (13)
Fairfax School

Night-Time's Here And Winter's Near

The rain falls down outside the window.
The cars drive by with lights so bright.
The sun has vanished out of sight.
The day gives up without a fight.

Daytime's gone and night-time's here.
The dark gives out the feeling of fear.
The moon's come out to meet the stars.
The wet road glistens in the light from the cars.

The radio in the room fades into the distance.
The room smells warm and full of Christmas.
With the house so cosy, inviting and warm
Winter creeps near without us knowing,
It's definitely here, the signs are showing.

Chapped lips and hands and cheeks so pink.
All you need is a nice hot drink,
To warm us up and keep us bright.
A cosy ending to the night.

Sophie Turner (13)
Fairfax School

Midnight In The Tree House

All alone in the tree house
In the middle of the night
All alone with cobwebs and the fading of the light.

See the owls sitting in the tree
Going hoot . . . hoot, hoot at me
Everything else . . . dead silence
Things feel so violent.

As the rain falls down to the ground
It makes a very loud sound
The moon glows a ghostly grey
And the bats' silhouettes go flitting away

The trees look like monsters
Coming to get me,
I feel so helpless, I scream
Help . . . me . . .

Sammy Kelland (12)
Fairfax School

SPELLBOUND

Witches on broomsticks all around,
All the spells are in a spellbound.
In the cauldron goes the frog.
Then the snail and the log.
To be a spell.
Says the witch
No more longer shall I itch?
Itching here and itching there.
No more itching I can bear.
Loopy loo, loopy lee.
That is how the spell should be.
The witches put on their black hats,
As they fly out the room with their big black cats.

The spell was all about today.
How the witches would get away.

Elia Islip (11)
Fairfax School

MIDNIGHT IN THE VILLAGE

When the lights have darkened
All the creatures crawl out
Nobody walking along the pavement
No boy no girl wandering about.

Now it's time for us to play
Creep instead of sleep
Run around and have our say
In the midnight moonlight.

So into the morning light
Out goes the darkness of the night
Back we creep out of sight
Until the morning light.

Kirsty Jones (12)
Fairfax School

MY CORNER

I am standing here.
Alone, in my corner
No one is allowed here.
If they are, it is either my best friend Stephanie
Or my white gerbils
I read books in my corner.
And eat chocolate chip cookies
But no one can share them with me
My corner has pink wallpaper and a white border
And chocolate marks of where I've made chocolate
                          patterns on the paper
I'm standing here in my corner,
My corner, all alone.

Anneliese Mountford (14)
Fairfax School

MIDNIGHT IN THE VILLAGE

Today in a little town called Spooksville,
There lived a ghost called Bones.
Bones loved scaring at the well,
Because of the crunching of bones.

The smell of blood is overwhelming,
From the rotting flesh.
Eyeballs pop out of a crushed skull,
Right onto my ghostly white vest.

Still by the well,
Bones look around.
Frightened to see.
A ghostly hound covered in blood.

They chase each other,
Around the well,
Both from another world,
Going to hell.

James Morris (12)
Fairfax School

REFLECTIONS

The rushes sway softly in the evening breeze.
The moon hangs in the opaque sky scattered with stars.
I looked in the calm lake and saw a duplicate likeness of me,
standing out in the stillness of the gloom.
My mind wandered from my aimless days of childhood,
to my contemplating long days of adulthood.
I re-lived my days of school,
on the field or working hard, full of blissful memories,
which will never fade like shadows when the sun blenches.

Philip Hamilton (12)
Fairfax School

MIDNIGHT IN THE BEDROOM!

Do you think your house is haunted
When it's dark and cold at night?
In the darkness do you tremble
At the sound of fighting ghosts?

Does your bed light hiss and curse
Or do your posters say 'Hello'?
Do you hide beneath the bed sheets
Praying for a brand new day?

Can you taste the dust balls flying?
Can you see the spider crawling?
Does your skin feel prickly all over
Or do you lie there like a statue?

On the floor you see a finger
You feel stiff, a shiver runs down you
Was that a mouse that you just saw
Swiftly dancing across the floor?

Your wardrobe opens and cackles a laugh
You're feeling nervous, it had a big mouth
Its big green eyes draw you nearer and nearer
Your body lies motionless as it gets
      pulled in with fear.

Mind-warping, knees knocking
     paralysed with fear
Hair-raising, bone-crackling
     numbness draws near.

Can you feel your sweat run down you?
A figure of ghostly white?
Can you hear the owl hooting?
Or do you lie there, teeth grinding?

As the morning comes alive
Your heart goes down to a steady pace
A mop of sweat clouds your head
You hear your mother lightly tread
Safe!

Nicole Dunn (12)
Fairfax School

MIDNIGHT IN THE COUNTRYSIDE

In the middle of nowhere,
Nothing to be seen,
Just fields and the birds,
It all seems so mean.

I hear the flapping round me,
Then came a rustle in the trees,
Still nothing in sight,
Nothing, nothing but the birds and bees.

An awful smell,
A bit like manure,
I think of horses but still nothing,
I hear a bell ring but I'm not so sure.

I feel really frightened,
I want to go home,
But I can't find a way of escaping,
I still wander, wander on my own.

A figure in the blackness,
My chance of getting away,
On a horse I jump we gallop into the darkness,
At home at last ready for the next day.

Angelina Rose (12)
Fairfax School

MIDNIGHT IN THE BASEMENT

Have you ever wondered how your basement looks at night
With a fading of a light.
When it's so dark and silent
And you're in for a massive fright.

Going down the stairs, creak, creak, creak,
Heard a mouse go by going squeak, squeak, squeak
Trying to find the light where can it be
Because in the dark I cannot see.

Going down the stairs can't find the light
Just missed a step Oh what a fright.
Head feeling hot, heart beating fast
Sweat pouring down I hope this doesn't last
My legs are just like jelly.
I feel like a floppy welly.

I've got goose-bumps on my arms
My hands feel all sticky
My body feels stiff
Er what's that horrible whiff
Smells like smoke I'd better get out
I do hope there's an extinguisher about.

Louise Matthews (12)
Fairfax School

A WITCH'S PARTY

Witches here,
Witches there,
Witches almost everywhere,
Potions, magic all fantastic now the witches
are getting erratic!
They jump, dance and prance.
As I watch from a bush,
they fly up high and do loop the loops on their brooms,
A witch's party and some of them look tarty even though
they're ninety!
They now descend,
but still the party does not end.
Some of their friends come and join,
even though it is almost ten!
Then they light a fire by looking in their spell books
and reading

> *'Frampaty Amp'*

Then again they prance and dance.
It is Hallowe'en in the early hours of the morning,
the witches fly away and migrate,
but someone has left a broom,
so I take it to my room,
fly out of the window to the high,
but oh dear I have lost the broom, oh no I'm going to die!
And what's even worse I landed on a spike,
the spike of the hat of the witch who had lost the broom!
She told me off and sent me to my room!

Chris Smith (11)
Fairfax School

SPELLBOUND

Witches, witches,
witches galore,
bats' wings, frogs' legs in the cauldron
they pour,

Bubble, bubble goes the steamy cauldron,
miaow, miaow goes the black cat,
cackle, cackle goes the wicked witch,

Dancing, dancing goes the cackling witch,
round her bubbling cauldron,
with her old spell book,
with her gruesome look,
she scares off all the children.

Ian Standley (11)
Fairfax School

SPELLBOUND

I enter the garden where the witches fly at night,
on their broomsticks they whiz! Whiz! Whiz!
Fleas in their hair,
fleas in their tea,
they eat them all the time and become something
like a witch,
they are terrifying and scary.
I walked into their home,
I got invited to have a cup of tea,
and to my surprise there were fleas in my tea.
It is so scary.

Kirsty Cotterill (11)
Fairfax School

MIDNIGHT IN THE UNIVERSE

Floating,
Through the open darkness of the night,
Teeth chattering, spine crawling,
Hair-rising chill down my spine,
See a spine-crawling, body-shivering,
Brain-shaking movement through the
                dark mist of the night.

The movement is a black figure,
Silence follows,
My whole world dissolves into the darkness,
The figure fades like the clouds move.

Floating through the open darkness of the night,
Floating through the dim light of the night,
The figure fades with a decaying smell.

Adam Bennett (12)
Fairfax School

THE DEEP DARK NIGHT

On the deep dark night of Hallowe'en
The witches laugh but are never seen.
Witches with broomsticks do fly high,
Till back in their beds the witches do lie.
Flying fast to find a bit of trouble,
Wanting, wanting to say 'Hubble, bubble!'
The black cat hissing and clawing,
The strong, strong magic stops from falling.
When the night is over the witches feel so blue.
But as for all the other people they just say *'Phew!'*

Mandy Richards (11)
Fairfax School

POLLUTION THROUGH THE EYES OF A CHILD

Changing from city to countryside,
I think is brill.
Hearing on the news people have died,
I'm glad I'm not there still.
They died through pollution
There must be a must be a solution.

You're breaking down the ozone,
Letting in harmful rays.
Killing us down to the bone,
So my teacher says.

The government is doing nothing
But listen to someone sing,
It's up to the people now,
But how?

You're breaking down the ozone,
Letting in harmful rays.
Killing us down to the bone,
So my teacher says.

I shall not forget about all of this,
Because pollution is not absolute bliss.
Can the world have no pollution?
Is there a solution?

You're breaking down the ozone,
Letting in harmful rays.
Killing us down to the bone,
So my teacher says.

This horrid stuff is done by cars,
People travelling to bars.
Don't go out for a drink,
Get it from the sink.

Katy Pemberton (12)
Fairfax School

MIDNIGHT IN A GRAVEYARD

While wandering through a graveyard
Very late tonight,
I heard a noise, I turned around,
And got an awful fright.
There behind the bushes,
An eerie figure stood,
The moon shone down,
And lit the ground,
And I could see the blood.

For there before my very eyes,
It stood so still and tall,
I dare not move or take a breath,
For fear that I should fall,
It slowly moved towards me,
And I can see its face,
A chill that ran,
Right down my spine,
And made my heartbeat race.

The body is disfigured,
Such an awful sight,
I knew I had to get away,
And run off into the night.

Laura Green (12)
Fairfax School

SPELLBOUND

The black cat was sitting on the back of the broom
Flying up to the bright full moon,
The witch was cackling all the time,
Singing this the witches' rhyme,
The witch was picking her dirty warts, verrucas,
                              pimples and all sorts,
The broomstick was enjoying himself
                    flying through the wood,
Watching the night as much as he could,
The moon was getting nearer and nearer,
The craters on it were getting clearer,
When they get there what will they do?
They will scare everyone even you,
So before they get you try and hide,
Or in her cauldron you might be fried,
So if I were you I'd watch out,
Because there are a lot of nasty people about,
Vampires, witches and devils,
Mixing their spells with lizard tails,
The witch is trying to make long nails,
And that is the end of my incredible tales.

Anne-Marie Tarver (11)
Fairfax School

MIDNIGHT IN THE GRAVEYARD

Midnight in the graveyard is very dark indeed
With spooky sounds and spooky smells
And flesh rotting away.

Eyes peeping through the bush
Arms hanging out the ground.
Twigs snapping, leaves crushed.
The dead are coming back!

Pale-white skin, blood red, bubonic brown
Colours you'd see around the graveyard.
Hear the moans of the dead piercing your ear.

Howling wolves chewing on flesh and bone
Screaming voices at the horrible sight
The dead are coming back!

Ben Webster (12)
Fairfax School

MIDNIGHT IN THE CASTLE

Have you ever imagined . . . ?
A dark haunted castle
Standing all alone
The sun is setting down below
Owls are hooting to and fro.

Inside it's dark and cold
Coat of armour standing old
Pictures, statues on the wall
All jump out to give a roar.

It's all completely pitch black now
The castle is out of sight,
Thunder and lightning lights the inside
But it is still black outside.

*Crack! G*oes the thunder
And gives a big fright
And breaks the stillness of the night.

Natalie Hull (12)
Fairfax School

MIDNIGHT IN THE SLAUGHTER HOUSE

In the day as pigs and cows are slaughtered
The blood trickles along the floor.
Just wonder what it would look like *at night.*

The door opens,
A loud creak echoes around the room.
Rats chewing on bones
The loud hum of the refrigerator.

Suddenly from behind the refrigerator
A loud *bang!*
And a man falls to the floor.
Rats scurry and disappear,
More blood runs along the floor,
And trickles down into the large hollow drain.

The loud, clear ring of the sirens
Came from far away;
Rats started feeding on the fresh body,
Sirens getting *closer* and *closer,* then . . .

James Simkins (12)
Fairfax School

SPELLBOUND

Ugly witches flying through the dark night,
Looking to give someone a nasty fright,
Hocus, pocus diddrog, turn that man into a frog,
All the witches laughed and cried,
Fell off their broomsticks and died,
The spell was broken in a flash,
The man was left with a green rash.

Stephanie Tisdale (11)
Fairfax School

MIDNIGHT IN THE GRAVEYARD

Here alone in a dark graveyard
Lying alone an empty box
Full of bones and rotten ashes
All covered in dust.

There lies a coffin
All smothered in mud
With wiggly worms and creepy crawlies
Catching the midnight's dusk.

Footsteps walking along the path
Tingling chains that make me shiver
All that runs straight down my back
A big black bird gave me a fright.

Rupinder Kaur (12)
Fairfax School

SPELLBOUND

Witches cackling
bones rattling
the witches come out to play
they lark about
they mess around making lots of sound
they're up all night giving people a fright.
You feel a gush of wind go past you
what's that?
It's them
it's them, it's the witches come out to play.

Jamie Ward (11)
Fairfax School

MIDNIGHT IN YOUR BEDROOM

Could you ever imagine
What happens at night,
When you're fast asleep
Quite warm, nice and tight.

The wind whistles loudly
In the light of the moon,
You drop to sleep
In silence, quite soon.

Slowly and quietly
Your room comes awake,
Then come the grumbles,
From the long-ending day.

Although you don't know it
Your hair stands on end,
As your teddies take footsteps
And talk of your friends.

Your posters rustle
Then jump off the wall,
Boyzone and Hanson
Spice Girls and all.

The sun starts to rise
In the eastern sky,
Everything gets back into place
Your books and pens fly.

Wait until another night
When the day has passed through,
Remember what I've said
As all this is true.

Gemma Clarke (12)
Fairfax School

Spellbound

Silence as I walk along the path, twisting towards the witch's house,
where usually there are unusual noises,
magical sparks,
and where there are broomsticks and black cats,
witches and wizards, ghosts and ghouls.
Now, just silence, pure silence.

Slowly I creep up to the door,
Bang!
Now the broomsticks fly again, cats miaow and howl again
witches, wizards, ghosts and ghouls
come out of their hiding places, dance around for five minutes
then *silence* once again.

Holly Lewis (11)
Fairfax School

Spellbound

Witches ride on wooden brooms swiftly
through the night, mysterious things in
castles they'll give you such a fright.
Creaky floors and squeaky doors.
Frightening screams, you'll get scary
                                          dreams.

So I would stay inside!

Luke Renfrew (11)
Fairfax School

MIDNIGHT IN THE BEDROOM

People have you ever been scared of . . .
The sight of your bedroom at night?
When everything is silent
When there is no more light.

You hear a great big crash
And your skin gets covered in goose-bumps
You wait a little while
As they turn into bigger lumps.

You slowly pull your quilt down
And boy do you get a surprise
When all the shadows jump at you
And your heart nearly dies.

You feel a sticky warmth
Run down your little forehead
And you realise
That your colour is blood-red.

Sniff . . . sniff
And smell something quite weird
You feel around and find the smell
 is really nothing
Just . . . *nothing*.

You feel really scared
You don't want to wait
In case you get another scare
And end up on a plate.

Stephen Gater (12)
Fairfax School

MIDNIGHT IN THE BARN

If barns are scary in the daylight,
Just think of what they're like at night,
All those rats scurrying by,
Well it gave me quite a fright.

All the shadows on the wall,
The smell of rotting hay,
Hear the wind howling outside,
Will I ever find the way?

Walking very slowly now,
Through the barn alone,
Thinking all the time,
Wishing I was at home.

All the tractors laugh at me,
Squeaking as they go,
A bat swooped down before me,
And I jumped back in terror.

Starting to speed up again,
The birds are also singing,
Approaching the exit now,
My head is really ringing.

The sun is rising in the sky,
Hooray! It's the next morning,
I don't want to go through that again,
Unless there is a warning.

Dan Wells (12)
Fairfax School

Midnight In The Hall

Hearing sounds from the stairs
Click, click, click!
Calling out to my mum
No answer!

At the top of the stairs thinking
All that happens is that hairs stand on end
Moving down the stairs the banister wobbling.
I'm wobbling too.

Shadows in the moonlight
Howls from the kitchen
Radiators rattling
Clocks ticking, tick, tick, tick!

Something was moving, quickly,
                        dodging things in sight
Hearing screams from the clock
Tapping on the floor
Misty grey steam, by my feet.

I'm walking towards the steam
Then I'm running
It's steam from a fire
            but where?

Simon Gore (12)
Fairfax School

SPELLBOUND

As the witches lurk through the night,
I get scared,
As I go through the woods,
I see a bush rustle,
It is a black cat.
As I look ahead of me I see a rotten
old house,
I carry on and knock on the door,
And who's there to greet me?
A pack of cackling witches,
Their cauldron so black,
Their red-eyed cat
Their vase full of dead roses,
Their shelves packed with frogs' legs.
As I walk through the woods,
I get scared,
I see another house,
But it's nothing to worry about,
It's my own house,
Hang on, what's that in the window?
Ash! It's just mom playing about in
                            the window,

    Or is it?

James Moore (11)
Fairfax School

WITCHES

The black cat walks at night,
With his owner on his right,
The moon and stars shine out light,
So they can find their way to Spooky Towers,
It's Hallowe'en and everyone calls out,
Trick or Treat,
Black pointed hats and cauldron full of frogs,
With broomsticks, potions and spells.

Vicky Yau (11)
Fairfax School

DEDICATED TO DIANA, PRINCESS OF WALES

To a dear Diana,
Your love was so great,
Our 'People's Princess'
Who met a terrible fate,
A woman who had
So much love in her heart,
The pain was unbearable,
When we had to part,
The world feels so cold,
Without you to hold,
Your beauty, your grace,
We can never replace,
You cared about others,
You were everyone's mother,
Goodnight and God bless
To our 'People's Princess'.

Victoria Rocks (11)
Great Wyrley High School

SUMMER IN BLOOM

The blazing sun beats down from a clear blue sky,
As the young birds glide and fly,
Tempting smells of barbecues float past.
Out come the refreshments, food at last!
Heavenly ice-cream, as soft and white as snow,
Causing smiles on children's faces to show.

The ants march on their parade course,
And the bees fly by - the bugs' 'air force'!
As the lawnmowers in the distance quietly hum,
People smile, nobody's glum.
The comforting sun will sleep soon,
As I relax in the hot summer noon.

David Mouatt (16)
Great Wyrley High School

CANDLE IN THE WIND

The loss is a great one which no one can explain,
Nothing can describe all the hurt and the pain,
Although I never knew you,
I saw your radiant glow,
As you visited the dying
And sick, that was not for show,
And now as I sit and watch the news,
And hear it on the radio,
This is the only news I do not wish to know,
That now our 'Queen of Hearts' has been taken from us all,
This is the worst news that I can ever recall.
God bless Diana.

Katie Pawlowski (13)
Great Wyrley High School

THE WITNESS
*(Based on the events of Macbeth's second
meeting with the witches in Shakespeare's 'Macbeth')*

      As they uttered the names of substances foul,
And flung them down into the hole,
      Lightning flashed, thunder boomed,
And smoke of purple and green,
      Flew from the pit, where the witches did sit,
Such proof of God's rage, I'd never seen.
      The trees seemed alive, and appeared to reach down,
Almost blocking the sight of the sky.
      Only the moon and the storm clouds above,
Could be seen from where I did reside.
      Suddenly, a figure emerged from the trees,
Cloaked, but more human than the rest.
      Yet something *even more* evil hung around him,
And to my horror it was . . . *King Macbeth!*
      What was he doing here? What had he to do,
That could possibly include these three fiends?
      He was a tyrant I knew, but could it really be true,
That he relies on these hags for his schemes?
      And if he confides with creatures like this,
What else happens, hidden by stealth?
      Perhaps there's more that has not been revealed,
Perhaps he's not human himself.

James Wilton (16)
Great Wyrley High School

THE FIRE DANCE

Annual autumn arrives,
Our eyes see trees made bare,
By the brisk brittle breeze
That make the fire fairies fall.
Fluttering and flapping,
Crisping and cracking,
The fire fairies fall.

The wind whips whilst I walk,
My body shivers cold,
My eyes burn seeing fire
Crimson, cocoa and copper.
Fluttering and flapping,
Crisping and cracking,
The fire fairies fall.

Orchards flourish, apples bloom,
Cherry, ruby and rose.
The crisp crunch in a bite
Smell sweet redolent air as,
Fluttering and flapping,
Crisping and cracking,
The fire fairies fall.

Jennifer Smith (15)
Great Wyrley High School

THE PEOPLE'S PRINCESS

Disaster struck one Saturday eve,
The earth, friends and family she did leave,
The worst national tragedy since Kennedy,
The world grieved for the most
photographed lady.

The 'People's Princess' loved and cared for
the common man,
The myths she did ban,
About the people with the terrible
disease - Leprosy.

She presented awards and gave speeches,
She smiled for the cameras on the beaches,
She loved her sons like any mother would,
She spent as much time with them as she could.

So why was it that on August 30th 1997,
The 'People's Princess' was taken to heaven?

Emma Foster (15)
Great Wyrley High School

THE BARN OWL

A barn owl's front is ghostly white.
She quarters the land in silent flight.
With black soulless eyes that pierce the night.

Her talons so lethal, and with hearing so keen.
A bird that is regal, as proud as a queen.
She swoops on her prey, never heard, never seen.

Natalie Hall (16)
Great Wyrley High School

YOU WILL BE LOVED
(A tribute to HRH Prince William and
HRH Prince Harry
on the tragic loss of their mother
Diana, Princess of Wales)

Don't be afraid to shed your tears,
Don't be afraid to show your fears,
In a heart is where you shall be
And special is what you will always be.

You will be loved in many ways,
Living on in you is where she will stay,
So don't have fear, for someone will be near,
You will be loved.

Trying to understand what you are going through,
Is not the easiest thing to do,
But you were bold, brave and above all,
You showed great strength, now you're admired
by all.

You will be loved in many ways,
Living on in you is where she will stay,
So don't have fear, someone will be near,
You will be loved.

Now it's time to hold your head up high,
She's on her way to freedom, it's time to say goodbye,
But we'll be there beside you, each and every day,
A hand to hold, a stepping stone, a friend in every possible way.

You are loved in many ways,
Living on in you is where she will stay,
So don't have fear, someone is here.
You are loved.

Natalie Till (15)
Great Wyrley High School

STROLL IN THE CITY

I wander alone in the shadows, unnoticed,
through the intricate web of veins in the city,
Surrounded by people like blood cells
Who rush along to their destinations.
Waste, digested food, blocks the arteries
and clings to my feet like melted tar.
Beside me the town's blood gushes;
Cars seem to swim in a fast-flowing river
that brings life to this slumbering giant.
It exerts its only effort;
It belches the waste of the town out
through its huge, pouting concrete mouth.
The cells disperse into organs.
The only movement is rhythmic breathing.
I hear the hushed hum of the lungs
as I wander alone in the shadows, unnoticed.

Angela Hawkins (15)
Great Wyrley High School

MARK AND CRICKET

I once knew a boy called Mark
Who loved to play in the park
His favourite sport was cricket
But he couldn't hit the wicket
Even though he practised till dark.

Mark would practise night and day
And people came from far away
Amazingly he still loved cricket!
But then one day he hit the wicket
And the crowd that gathered cheered, 'Hooray!'

Mark was on a good run now
With all the onlookers going, 'Wow!'
He bowled the balls down one by one
The bails and stumps going, going, gone
Yes Mark had improved somehow.

Now Mark is playing for a team
Moving the ball off the seam
And there are hundreds of scouts
Wanting to know his whereabouts
And one day he'll accomplish his dream.

Peter Harris (15)
Great Wyrley High School

THE LONELY HEDGEHOG

He sets out bravely o'er the crop-filled fields,
His beading, button eyes blinking as he searches,
Ready for danger,
Ready for battle,
His spiky spines stretched unto their peak,
Camouflaged in shadows of darkness.
Trees tower high, allowing a darkening funereal cloud
To settle over all beneath them.
They tower high like huge buildings,
Growing up into the sky.
Then suddenly, approaching from the field, something came,
Roaring, howling and yelling with pain,
Belching smoke, spreading high, up, up, into the sky,
Though moving as fluently as speech.
A monster with shining eyes, like a dragon,
A dragon in its immensity eating all before it.

Victoria Evans (15)
Great Wyrley High School

THE MAN

Who is this man
This tall dark man?
Who walks about sweating,
Lost as a lamb.
This man so tall,
His shoes all worn,
With overgrown stubble,
And hair on his face,
He looks a disgrace.
Has he no pride
As he takes a huge stride?
Has he no family, no money, no life?
Has he no children, no job and no wife?
Has he no home
Only the streets to roam?

Who is this man
This lonely man?

*Who is that man,
That tall dark man?*

**Jenna Strange (13)
Great Wyrley High School**

TELEVISION

At night I go home
And I don't know if it's me
But once my homework's out the way
I always turn on the TV.

I skim through the channels
And there's so much to see
Drama, game shows, sci-fi
Documentaries and comedy.

I like to watch 'The X-Files'
'Due South' and 'Jack Dee'
I watch them all evening long
And only stop for my tea.

I watch the channels
3,4,5 and the BBC
One day I will stop watching it
Well, *possibly!*

Martin Popov (14)
Great Wyrley High School

PARENTS

Who understands parents?
Because I certainly don't.
All they ever say to me is,
'No you won't!'

I go home every night,
Only to find another fight.
Of course I love them and really care,
But they treat me very 'unfair'.

Because I am the oldest,
I always get the blame.
My brothers and sisters get off scot-free
And it will always be the same!

Amanda Pearce (16)
Great Wyrley High School

MY ONLY SECRET FROM YOU

When I see you
You are like artwork for my eyes only.
When I hear you
The sound of your voice lifts my soul to a feeling of intensity.
When I am near you
I close my eyes and feel your body heat radiate across to mine.
No one else is capable of cleansing my soul
Of the depression which lingers within.
Why is it that I am only ecstatic with you?
It riddles me that you aren't with me for infinity.
My love for you has nowhere to go -
It is trapped and unable to escape
Your satin caress leaves behind a burning trace of desire.
Your voice eats away at my heart
Taking a piece at every word spoken.
I try to imagine your body so strong,
Yet warm and gentle enclosing around mine at midnight
As I fall into tranquil slumber.
My fingers crave the experience of sensing your hair
With its delicate flex of moonshine.
I would risk my life
To prevent pain and anguish from harming you.
I admire your cares for all humanity;
I love your wish for harmony for all;
I cherish the way in which your face lifts
To another dimension when you smile;
I relish your sense of humour.
I adore the true, whole you -
I love you so immensely that not even poetry
Can describe the depth of my love for you.

Emma Spencer (15)
Great Wyrley High School

MISSION: SNOW

The shimmering sounds
Of the whistling curling wind
Made a diversion
For the eager, frost-biting,
Army of snow
That floated down
And drifted soundlessly,
Like people parachuting
From nowhere
With their crisp, white transparent uniform.
As the talcum powder soft snow
Softly made a blanket of glistening silk,
Plants fought in a combat zone
Of verdant green and fluffy pale white,
Trying not to become captive prisoners,
Like their ancient friends,
Who once lived
In the bitter, frozen Arctic.
Suddenly a blazing flicker
Of beaming yellow and fire-like red
Filled the dim, dusky, shimmering moonlit sky.
The army of snow slowly started to deteriorate
Into crunchy, dark brown slush.
For the sun had brought reinforcements
Of beaming flashes of yellowy light.
It melted like a mountainous decaying building,
Crumbling to the ground.
The snowflake army
Has failed its mission once again.

Richard Footman (15)
Great Wyrley High School

MY GARDEN

At dawn the roaring sun starts to rise,
A volcano of heat way up so high,
Brightening up my dismal land,
Making a magical change that may never die.

A whirlpool of colour now grows in my garden,
Twisting and twirling like a fairground ride,
Blooming out and filled with enchantment,
But dancing as though they've nothing to hide.

My babbling brook rushes past in excitement,
Gurgling, gushing and skipping along,
Darting like a hungry fox,
And splashing, scurrying, singing its song.

The fluffy clouds whisper and whistle softly,
Drifting through the new summer morn,
Peering down and seeing, in astonishment,
Fresh dewdrops fallen on the front lawn.

Soon my garden retreats to its dismal condition
As the ball of fire silently curls up and dies,
Reality is shown in the pale moonlight,
But the magical images are still reflected in my eyes.

Kerri Baker (15)
Great Wyrley High School

UNLUCKY

Mr Step wrote 'Falling Over'
'Cliff Disaster' by Eileen Dover
Luke Bothways got run over
What they need is a four-leaf clover.

Christopher Stokes (12)
Great Wyrley High School

THE FOUR SEASONS

In the springtime the sun comes up,
And a new fresh day dawns again.
Spring reminds me of flowers in bloom,
Buttercups, daisies and daffodils.
It also reminds me of little birds and insects,
Butterflies start flying around,
And little lambs come into life.

Summer comes and starts to get warmer,
Longer days and nights get shorter,
The hot sun rises and the holidays begin,
And people pack their suitcases and start to flee.
The sun is so bright and shining in our eyes,
Ladybirds and butterflies come into view,
And flowers grow in our gardens and make it look colourful.

Autumn's here and the nights close in.
I walk down the path on the crunchy leaves;
The red, brown and yellow leaves light up the path,
And make it look like a path on fire.
The weather has turned cold and windy.
The leaves fall off the trees and drop everywhere.

Winter's now finally arrived,
And November's come again, Guy Fawkes is here.
Bonfires and fireworks are shooting everywhere.
It is now really cold and bad weather has started.
Now the dark mornings are here,
And we are celebrating Christmas and New Year.
Snow starts to fall and puts a white sheet over the village.

The year is out and the seasons all start up again.

Laura Sensier (14)
Great Wyrley High School

DOLPHINS

Dolphins are my favourite animals,
I love to watch them swim;
All round the bay they go,
Never looking dim.
Then they go and perform,
Intelligent, and tame,
But then come hunters ready to kill.
Isn't it a shame?
Soon all of the dolphins are gone,
You'll never see them again now they're gone.
Is it worth it, seeing them dead?
Or would it be better seeing them
Swimming in the ocean again?
They only get one chance,
And now there is a price on their head,
Off the hunters go again,
The money keeps rolling in,
For a tail, a tooth or a fin.
They don't care,
Just as long as their pockets are never bare.

Emma Strange (12)
Great Wyrley High School

TIMELESS DREAM

As I climb the tiring stairs to bed,
After closing my hands and bowing my head,
My eyelids feel heavy, and as I recall,
My head on my pillow will soon slowly fall.

And now in a place where no one feels sad,
Where troubles are few, still no one is mad,
I fondly drift to a time in May,
With family and friends one enchanted day.

The smell of the air, and a garden of flowers,
The bright laughing faces that chortled for hours,
The night and the world looked on by the moon,
And that long summer day that was over too soon.

The new morning sun, through the window beams,
The loving bright faces still there in my dreams.
And that is a place where they always will stay,
Preserved in the memory, of that summer's day.

Sarah Robinson (15)
Great Wyrley High School

BLACK AND BLUE

What colour are my arms, black or blue?
How many bruises, one or two?
One and two and many more,
My feet are red and very sore,
I've bruises on my legs as well,
I told my Mum I'd slipped and fell.

Nasty names every day,
Why don't they stop and go away?
They'd hide my books just for play,
I don't know why they act this way,
Things they do and things they say,
I wonder what's in store for me today?

Time for school I don't feel well,
I really feel sick when I hear that bell,
The only way to escape this hell,
Someday, somehow I have to tell.

Lindsay Joynes (12)
Great Wyrley High School

DECORATING

Home life is great,
But can be in a state.
The kitchen's a mess,
The walls are coming down,
It looks better less and less,
Mum's got a frown.

Home life is great,
But can be in a state.
The hall's in a state,
Dad's trying to create,
Isn't life great!

Richard Armstrong (13)
Great Wyrley High School

THE JESTER

The jester is a funny man,
He has a golden tan.
He wears the funniest clothes I've ever seen,
And he's seen places I've never been.

I was told he went to the King,
The King thought the jester was going to sing.
But instead the jester pulled his nose,
And stood on his toes.

I heard the King put the jester in jail,
And that's from where he tells his tale.
I've not seen the jester for a while,
But when I think of him he makes me smile!

Laura Sutton (13)
Great Wyrley High School

ANIMALS

Deep, deep down at the bottom of the sea,
Fish, dolphins and whales are supposed to all swim free,
But they are captured and polluted by mankind,
Nothing else runs through their minds.

Animals deserve rights too,
What else are they supposed to do?

Elephants roam around the lands,
Their tusks are found in people's hands,
Protesters are right,
Some tigers are sad and will bite,
Why don't we just give them a break,
They are living in a world of hate.

Claire Parfitt (13)
Great Wyrley High School

BEING EVACUATED

Clutching my teddy bear tightly,
Waiting for the train to come,
My luggage sitting beside me,
Crying is my mum.

The train pulls up, it's time to go,
I am in tormenting pain,
I pick up my little leather suitcase,
And board the dirty train.

I wave goodbye,
My mother still crying,
I look out of the window,
No one smiling.

Joanne Nicholls (13)
Great Wyrley High School

NOVEMBER 5TH

Fireworks rise up to the sky,
With a fizz, pop, crack.
Reaching up like tiny hands,
Bright colours they never lack.

Colours of all sorts in the sky,
Turquoise, scarlet and lime.
Opening up like tiny flowers,
I'm amazed all of the time.

At last they light the huge bonfire,
It swells as big as a balloon,
The guy is immediately devoured,
It'll all be over soon.

Sparks drift down to the ground
Like softly dancing snow
Dancing about like the autumn leaves,
Then fade and die into darkness,
      It's time to go.

Michelle Morgan (12)
Great Wyrley High School

MY MIND IS BLANK

My mind is blank,
There's nothing there.
I'm submerged, I've sunk,
And my brain doesn't care.

What am I writing?
It doesn't make sense.
My bulbs need relighting,
Why am I so tense?

My head's a volcano,
Ready to explode.
Why won't my pen go?
Please give me the code.

Oh, who cares anyway,
My message won't be heard.
I'll maybe try another day,
With more inspiring words.

Amy Finney (13)
Great Wyrley High School

UNTITLED

Flowers line the streets of London
People stand in grief
The flowers make a floral ocean
In places six feet deep.
People mourning, paying their respects,
Not a dry eye in sight.
Queuing to sign the 'Books of Condolence'
All day and night.
Over Buckingham Palace
The flag flies at half-mast.
The Royal Family all in black,
Watch the hearse go past.
Raised upon the canon
You will remain deep in our hearts.
But now has come the time
When Diana has to part.

Claire Ramsdale (12)
Great Wyrley High School

LIFE SUPPORT

There's a lack of oxygen where I lie,
In my iron lung tonight,
I find it so very hard to breathe.
Would someone turn my life support system on,
'Cause I can't reach?
Please!
Another quiet hour alone,
In my iron lung tonight,
A tear runs slowly down my cheek.
Would someone turn my life support system on,
'Cause I can't reach?
Please!
Now I'm drowning in a river of my tears,
If all you say,
Is all there is,
Then stop because you are scrambling up my ears.

Stuart Gregory (12)
Great Wyrley High School

THE SONG

I close my eyes and open my heart,
The song that I sing is of a world being torn apart.
A world of war,
A world of hate,
A world where love,
Stands up to fate.
A distant hope like a faraway light,
A wish made upon a star at night.

A barricade that separates the people,
A torn flag that separates their hearts.

Louise Clare (13)
Great Wyrley High School

PAPARAZZI
(Peace, Love, Empathy)

Man prepared his ground,
And the seed of which became,
That of the first media picture being broadcast,
Who would know of the disgrace that would
hang over their heads?
Devils with their lenses will chase around
Innocent victims who can't make a sound!
These people have no lives.

Daniel James Wilson (13)
Great Wyrley High School

EVERY DAY

Every day I think of you,
And my heart aches as I do.
Why did you go away,
And leave me here alone to stay?

Up I get every day,
And I make time to pray
For your soul, I wish to see,
Next time God please take me.

In this world you get old and die.
In your world you never lie.
How I wish I could be with you,
And think of how you didn't come too.

And I know I will get through,
Just as long as I think of you.

Emma Woodward (14)
Great Wyrley High School

IF I WERE FAMOUS . . .

If I were famous what would I be?
Perhaps an actress in repertory,
A singer, a dancer, or even a clown,
Strutting my stuff in every town.

If I were famous what would I be?
Perhaps a queen of a foreign land,
With lots of servants to have at hand,
Oh what a life, for me this would be,
To have everything I wanted, and be
                      happy as can be.

Oh but if I were famous, what would I be?
Perhaps a doctor in a famous street,
Caring for all, for the sick people I meet,
Preserving life, which is so sweet.

Oh well I'm not famous, I'm just me,
Plain and ordinary as can be,
I'll work hard, and do my best,
No clowning around or time to jest.

Then perhaps one day I may be,
That famous person from *Great Wyrley!*

Sarah Walker (14)
Great Wyrley High School

UNTITLED

My sister's got a Tamagotchi.
It's driving me completely potty!
She's asking me to baby-sit.
If it bleeps I will feed it.

If it bleeps again I'm sure I'll kill it.
But I will never, never, never baby-sit.
In fact, I'll just leave it to die.
My sister will come back and cry.

Jamie Manson (13)
Great Wyrley High School

UNEXPECTATIONS

I sometimes wonder about life
'Unexpectations', surprises yet strife
Love that's so warm, thoughtful and kind
A generous person, a gift to find
Bundles of joy but drowned in sorrows
Thoughts that wander far
Daydreams and horrors.

I open my window, a summer's day
To drown all my unhappiness away
But then I look, look again
Trees swaying, a blustery day
Happiness has gone, gone far
But the love I have helps me get through
Those blustery days that come so new.

Mixed emotions that come to people
Hatred, generosity, kindness that's due.
I watch as pearl drops of rain fall down
Feeling that they're my life
Draining away till the sun comes out
And then springing up like you've just been born
Bringing new happiness to the world
Warmth, kindness, but most importantly love.

Gemma Botterill *(12)*
Great Wyrley High School

STARTING YEAR 9

Starting year 9 I've been quite good,
Done all my homework as I should.
Listened to teachers, done what they said,
Sometimes rewarded for using my head.

It's normally 'C's' and 'B's' that I get,
I haven't had an 'A' just yet.
My merit sheet is somewhat empty,
By the end of the year I shall have plenty.

English, science, maths too,
All these lessons I have to do.
Art, RE, geography as well,
Until I hear the ringing of the bell.

Mark Reece (13)
Great Wyrley High School

THE LAKE

There's a lake in the middle of the forest,
It sparkles in the heat of the sun.
The water stays calm and never gets rough,
Then down to the river it will run.

Down to the river the water has run,
Where the water dives and dashes.
Here there's never a quiet moment,
Then down to the sea it will run.

Down to the sea the water has run,
Where its journey comes to an end,
But this poem will always keep on going,
If you read it again and again.

Amy Sensier (12)
Great Wyrley High School

Pub

Guz to the pub a lot,
Drinks alcohol a lot,
Makes me brain rot,
I'm totally mad,
I'm insane,
Guess wot lads,
I've lost me brain,
'Aven't got a clue,
Wot I'm gonna do,
Need the loo,
An' I can't see the door anymore,
I think I'm drunk,
I've got an empty glass,
I dribble out, *'beer'*,
Can't go to the bar,
'Cos I can't stand up,
I can't drive home,
Me mates won't let me steer,
I think I'll sleep in the pub cellar,
And look after the beer,
It's safer there than home,
'Cos me Mum's at home,
An' wot's she gonna say,
Me bein' fourteen,
An' out drinkin' all day,
Taxi comes,
I insult 'im a lot,
Guess wot,
I'm grounded!

Mark Bartlam (13)
Great Wyrley High School

HORIZON OF THE SUN

The sun that rises in the sky,
Isn't what it seems,
It's not just one huge brandy ball,
Or an excuse to eat ice-creams.

The sun is what makes life live,
And roses grow to bloom,
For animals to frolic in the fields,
Or an escape from night-time gloom.

The light is life,
The heat will save,
These rays of hope,
Will save our days.

Nichola Arrowsmith (12)
Great Wyrley High School

DIANA, QUEEN OF HEARTS

Death spears a wound no one can heal,
But memories are a treasure no one can steal.
Diana, you touched the hearts of the nation,
Having you gave us a warm sensation.
Many did not appreciate
The work you did, the love you donated.
We will miss you forever more
But for your work there's much in store.
We loved your work for charity,
Your work was clear to see,
Now I'll end this poem as it starts,
Goodbye Diana, 'Queen of Hearts'.

Gavin Wheatley (14)
Great Wyrley High School

PRINCESS DIANA

She was a 'Queen' to all her people,
Black or white, ill or fit,
No matter how famous or common.
She was a rose among all others,
She did things straight from the heart.
Poor William and Harry will never forget
The fabulous times they had.
Now she is gone,
To a place where no one can harm her.
She was the cream in our coffee,
The apple of our eyes,
She is forever in our hearts
And will always be remembered.
Princess Diana the 'People's Princess'
And the 'Queen of Hearts'.

Lisa-Marie Bowker (12)
Great Wyrley High School

QUEEN OF MY HEART

I would have loved to have met her,
It would have been a dream come true,
With her hair of blonde and eyes of blue.
All the charities she helped - there are too many to say,
But there's no doubt she thought of them every day.
With two sons of her own who loved so dear,
She went out to others to take away their fear.
With a loving hug and a caring smile,
She spread peace and happiness over many a mile.

Sonia Adshead (12)
Great Wyrley High School

The Ghost Girl

The house stood alone in the dark lane,
Never anyone around.
People have told me the story of the 'Ghost Girl'
Holding a small lamp,
I think I've seen it,
Small but bright,
So I decided to go and see the house
That people nicknamed the 'Ghost's Home'.
I walked slowly towards it and took a deep breath,
And peered through the window with all my courage.
There I saw my answer
In all her full glory,
Holding a small lamp.
The 'Ghost Girl'.
She walked around looking for something,
With her long, shimmering, golden hair,
And twinkling sky-blue eyes,
But as I looked closer she had disappeared.
Gone without a trace.

Jenine Fellows (12)
Great Wyrley High School

My Dad's Car

My dad's car is a Rover,
He tries to keep it clean.
With a turbo-charged engine,
It's a real mean machine.

No dogs allowed in his car,
The hairs would drive him mad,
No bags of crisps, no sweets, no drinks,
It's really rather sad.

The weekend comes with a bucket and sponge,
And a hose-pipe at the ready,
He works so hard for hours on end,
He ought to take it steady.

The car is now immaculate,
So I must not complain,
But poor old dad, the sky's gone grey,
I think it's going to rain.

Richard Nicholls (12)
Great Wyrley High School

WEST HIGHLAND WHITE TERRIER
(Dedicated to Whisky)

Eyes like lead in a snowbound head,
   See the life despite what I said,
Puppy look, born to be free,
   Taken to live domestically.

See him sleeping in midday,
   Wishing all his dreams away,
His ears stand as he hears the sound,
   His head rises as he comes around.

A small life in a big, wide world,
   But he doesn't care, he lives in a whirl,
See him play in the hills afar,
   He doesn't even know who his parents are.

Does he hide his worries behind a wagging tail?
   Does he cry in silence with an unheard wail?
I look at him and I feel so sad,
   That for me he gave up his mum and dad.

Lee Goodall (11)
Great Wyrley High School

TREACLE, MY SPECIAL BUNNY

Treacle just sitting there without a care,
She stood out among the rest,
What caught my eye, her golden chest.
Her big brown ears and big brown eyes,
They gave me a big surprise.
Her tiny nose twitching up and down,
Smelling who I was and I saw her frown.

Her mother was sitting proud and tall,
When Treacle's brother gave her a call.
Her father as big and black as night,
Her mother was small and golden bright.

I had to take her without a doubt,
So I fetched the box and picked her out,
On the way back home
She sat silent and restful
And curled up without a moan,
We took her in to her brand new home
Where again she adapted without a groan.

Now she has grown, still golden brown,
Tall and proud of her young ones now.

Emily Cartwright (12)
Great Wyrley High School

WHY, WHY?

Why did you go?
Was it just fate,
Or even the press?
Who did kill you that night?

You were the cream in our coffee,
The 'Queen of Hearts',
And the 'People's Princess'.

Bouquets of flowers have been laid,
Now the wilted are changed
Into compost but the fresh are
Kept to show your grace.

Why did you go?
Was it just fate,
Or even the press?

Krysia Baker (12)
Great Wyrley High School

WHAT A DOG!

Look at that dog!
It's big, it's mean, it's really scary,
Oh no it's black and tan and hairy.
It's got big sharp teeth
Which look like a sharp wreath.
Oh no it's coming towards me!
Probably to kill me.
Run like the wind,
Snap like the King,
Click my fingers,
Tell it to heel,
Help!
Scream, scream, scream!
It's on top of me,
Oh no! It's going to bite me.
Er, er, er, it's licking me,
Mum can we keep it?
That bushy-tailed dog.
We named her Sheba.

Jemma Moran (11)
Great Wyrley High School

God

Do I believe in God or not?
Did God create the world or not?
Stories I have been told,
Some seem new and some seem old.
Did Jesus turn water into wine?
Was the world made in seven days' time?
Is there a heaven? Is there a hell?
Is there anybody out there who can tell?
Are the stories I hear true
Or are they all lies?
Did God give Mary that special gift?
Can somebody give me a clue?
So many questions.
So many answers.
Which are true?
Which are false?
Now can you see why I'm not sure
Whether to believe or not?

Gemma Biddulph (11)
Great Wyrley High School

Time

Time is all around us,
Seconds, minutes, hours, days.
We set our lives around it,
In our little ways.

Grandfathers and watches,
All go tick, tick, tock.
Alarms and digital,
Are all clocks.

Tick tock, tick tock,
Goes Big Ben.
On the hour, every hour,
Even at ten.

Twelve o'clock, is lunchtime,
And that's what my watch says.
I'd better go to lunch,
In my own little way.

Helen Fleming (12)
Great Wyrley High School

WHAT ARE WE DOING TO OUR WORLD?

Cutting down trees,
Making little birds homeless,
Just because we want paper and nice comfy furniture,
Even though we're losing oxygen,
What are we doing to our world?

Dropping litter instead of putting it in our pockets,
Making our wildlife suffer,
Making our school look untidy,
What are we doing to our world?

Get into the car on a frosty morning,
Never thinking of walking or biking,
Filling the air with carbon monoxide,
Never thinking that your children are suffering
From your car fumes,
What are we doing to our world?

Charlotte Wood (12)
Great Wyrley High School

SISTERLY LOVE

When Mum's about to go to work,
She always explains to us,
'Now do the dishes, clean your rooms
And please don't make a fuss!'

So the moment she's stepped out of the door,
My sister glares at me,
I ask her, 'What's the matter?'
And she replies, 'You'll see.'

'Now don't think you're getting out easily,
'Cause you're doing all the work.'
And just when I'm about to run,
She pulls me back with a jerk.

So I have to do all the chores,
While she lounges around,
And I am busy working,
Until the doorbell sounds.

She grabs a duster and polish,
And pushes me out the way,
So it looks like she's been working
Busily all day.

So I go on and let Mum in,
And she walks around looking amazed,
Commenting on this and that,
And she gets all the praise!

Emily Brown (12)
Great Wyrley High School

SIGN OF WINTER

As the summer season closes in
A sign of winter appears.
Chillness from the northerly wind
Groaning in scary leers.

Darkness comes early
Swallowing up the light,
The frost sparkles with glitter
Sprinkling whiteness in the night.

Children go in with shorts and T-shirts
Come out again in jumpers and trousers,
It's the season of coldness
With icicle patterns on the windows.

The first fall of snow, falls on the ground
And the soft crunch of walking is the only sound,
Everywhere shows softness
All coloured with whiteness in a huge mound.

A snowman can be seen with his scarf and hat.
Children dancing around him full of laughter,
Along comes Jack Frost and with a touch you'll see -
The snowman then smiles with glee.

When Christmas comes, children are filled with delight
And open their presents in the candlelight,
As they gaze up at the Christmas tree
They say, *'Merry Christmas!'* to you and me.

Victoria Dean (11)
Great Wyrley High School

THE DAY WE SAID GOODBYE

Today's the day we say goodbye,
We shed a tear and start to cry.
I can't believe you've gone away,
I can't believe you're not here to stay.
When I see you in my head,
I want to tell you words unsaid.
Even though you've gone away,
In my heart you'll always stay.
Today's the day we say goodbye,
But in my heart you'll never die.
If I could see you just once more,
There are so many things I couldn't ignore.
But, now that you have gone,
I'll just have to use the memories of you
That I have inside.
So to Di what can I say?
I loved you then I love you now.
A part of you will never go,
Even though time goes slow.
Today's the day we say goodbye,
We all love you,
That's no lie.

Andrew Hulme (12)
Great Wyrley High School

A POEM ABOUT DIANA

She used to walk among the crowds,
Just blended with the usual sounds,
But she was something special;
The *Princess of Wales*.

She did so much for others,
She put them first,
She thought of her sons;
The *Princess of Wales*.

Matthew Fletcher (12)
Great Wyrley High School

LIFE

I think that people should live longer,
Than the life expectancy.
Everything you do until 75 is . . .
A natural urgency!

When you're a baby you learn to talk,
When you're a toddler you begin to walk,
When you're three you start play school,
When you're four you start nursery,
And when you're eleven you start the nightmare -
All you have is homework, homework and more homework.

You can either leave school at sixteen or . . .
Go for another two years and then
You start another school called 'university'.

Then you leave uni to go and start your new career,
Make lots of money, retire,
And sleep in front of the fire.

People shouldn't get old and grey,
They should stay young forever,
And die at the age of a hundred and fifty,
Then they could see how much things have changed
Since they were at school in the year 1850.

Siobhan Connolly (12)
Great Wyrley High School

TREASURED MEMORIES

I am luckier than many,
As I met Princess Di,
When I heard the awful news,
I had to sit and cry.
She was elegant and gentle,
She shared her love,
With those who have none.
I cannot believe,
Our 'Queen of Hearts' has really gone.

For me, like all of her people,
In our hearts she will always stay.
But I gave the Princess flowers,
I will treasure the memories of that day.

Amy Smith (12)
Great Wyrley High School

SWEETS

Lovely lips,
Sherbet dips,
Rabbit nips,
Spicy sips,
Snickers rips,
Toffee strips,
Lemon pips,
But most of all,
I love
the beautiful,
delicious,
Walnut
Whips.

Sarah Lewis (11)
Great Wyrley High School

BACK TO SCHOOL

Today is the first day of our holiday,
No more school for weeks.
I don't know what to do,
Might go to my friends,
Might go to the zoo,
Might go to the park, play till it's dark,
Might stay inside and write a book,
Might rain all week. That's just my luck!
Might go to McDonald's or Burger King,
Might go to town and buy a ring,
Might go to the pictures or ride my bike.
I fell off last night, and gave Mum a fright.
Might go to the baths for a splash.
The bus leaves in minutes so I must dash.
Might go to the match to see City win.
When they do my Dad makes a terrible din.
Two weeks isn't long to fit all this in -
There's homework to do and practising,
Baths to have, hair to wash,
Lots to get ready so we must rush.
Mum says, 'Come on, come on, come on, you fool.
It's time to get up!
And *go back to school.*'

Vicky Barrow (11)
Great Wyrley High School

My Favourite Person Is . . .

My favourite person is my Nan,
She's really kind and caring.

She gives me a lot of pleasure,
And calls me her little treasure.

She reminds me of some roses,
The way she stands there and poses.

She's a lady filled with love,
She's got everything a child could dream of.

She's the best Nan,
No one will ever be better than her.

There's only one Nan like mine,
That's why I've written this rhyme.

Zoe Teale (11)
Great Wyrley High School

Diana, Princess Of Wales

She was here,
Now she's gone.
The car was racing.
The press were waiting.
Diana and Dodi were killed.
Everyone was crying.
Diana had died.
All we can say is goodbye.

Lucia Grennan (11)
Great Wyrley High School

THE WAND

My little sister found a wand,
And she thought it was a doll.
She tapped it on the table,
And suddenly she was gone.

She turned up in Never Never Land,
With Peter Pan and Wendy.
She learned to fly and fight,
And killed Captain Hook last night.

My little sister found the wand again,
And tapped it on the tree.
Suddenly she vanished,
Back into her bed.

Lawrence Garbett (12)
Great Wyrley High School

POLLUTION

Yuck! Eurgh!
Sewage, chemical waste,
Travelling down into the ocean
In a slimy, thick, disgusting paste.
Killing animals, destroying trees,
Pumping our nasty concoctions
Into the seas;
You know we should stop!

Katy Owen (12)
Great Wyrley High School

MYSELF

Hi! I'm Lucy
I like computers
But I'm not very good at them
I like running
I know I'm good at that
I like horses
But I haven't got one *yet!*
I'm not too good at maths
But I'm OK
I'm OK at languages too.

Some people think I'm really, really cute!
I'm not sure about that though
I haven't got bright blue eyes
I've just got plain brown ones
But I'm not bothered about that.

I've got short, light brown hair
I've got a big smiley smile
And clean white teeth!

And that's all the things about me.

Lucy Ansell (11)
Great Wyrley High School

MY PET

I have a little furry friend,
I feed her every day,
I give her maize and oats to eat,
As well as lots of hay.

She's rather cute and cuddly,
And doesn't need much room,
She's lots of fun to play with,
And very easy to groom.

If the weather's nice outside,
I put her in her run.
She nibbles on the nice green grass,
And does have lots of fun.

I can hold her in my hands,
She isn't very big,
As you've probably guessed by now,
My pet's a guinea pig!

Jenny Hunt (11)
Great Wyrley High School

THE EAGLE

The eagle swoops along the sky
Staring down with his unblinking eye
Suddenly he was trapped in a cage
He looked longingly up at the sky.

Then a lady came in
And fed him old scraps out of the bin.
She said 'What a horrible bird!
No I think *ugly* is the word.'

The cage was opened
The bird was set free
Away he flew so elegantly
Perhaps I was wrong to call him *ugly*.

Jenny Tibbitts (11)
Great Wyrley High School

HAIRY FACES!

I've seen some hairy-faced men,
Who looked as though they were cavemen,
They could be called Den or Len,
Or just have a name like most men.

With hair all over your face,
You probably couldn't see to race,
But finally at last,
You could run fast,
If you had the hair taken off your face.

Is there a problem with shaving?
Or is there one with behaving?
But then when they buy
A razor, they think they'll die.

Adam Rolls (11)
Great Wyrley High School

THE SEA

When the sea roars
It could be a lion
Pouncing from rock to rock
Playing with the waves.

When the sea's slow
It could be a snake
Slithering round
To trap you
Making you run
To higher ground.

Tara Bevan (11)
Great Wyrley High School

SIMPLY FRED

A family in Canada once one day said,
'I think we'll move and leave the cat, Fred,'
Then one hundred weeks later,
Surprisingly, when you think of a cat's feline nature,
He was found in a heap on the mat!
1,995 miles,
Blimey!
That was sure to have taken a long while!
But now once again he's safe and sound,
Until . . .

A family in Canada once one day said,
'I think we'll move and leave the cat, Fred.'

Meow w w w!

Sarah Williams (11)
Great Wyrley High School

QUEEN OF HEARTS

She had lovely big eyes,
And a heart of gold.
She touched the hearts of all people,
Whether ill, young or old.
She was beautiful and pretty,
But now she sleeps at rest.
She'll always be the 'Queen of Hearts',
Diana was the best.

Kirsty Smith (11)
Great Wyrley High School

The First Day

My first day of school,
I'm nervous,
Shivering and shaking,
And before you say,
I wasn't cold at all
It was all right in the end,
And I have made lots of new friends.

Lynne Woodcock (11)
Great Wyrley High School

Princess, We Miss You

Princess, Princess, now you are gone,
What will we do?
We must carry on.
All the joy,
And the sorrow you gave us.
We've got nothing else to do.
We can only think of you.

Adrian Bullock (11)
Great Wyrley High School

My Special Aunt (Connie)

'Viking Con', that's her name,
And history is her game.
From George I to Henry IV,
And myths and legends with the minotaur.

She helps us with our work from school,
She's not stupid or a fool.
Once we've finished we take it home,
Before we leave we'll give Zac a bone.

Leanne Reece (11)
Great Wyrley High School

DIANA

Dear Diana, why did you have to go?
Everyone loved you so.
You'll always be the 'Queen of Hearts',
No one wanted us to part.
Like a flower that now has wilted,
You were a lady very gifted.
So Diana, it's time to say goodbye,
I know in our hearts you'll never die.

Harry Peake (11)
Great Wyrley High School

THE FORK-LIFT TRUCK

We need you fork-lift truck,
For jobs that we can't do,
Like carrying things and fetching things,
But sometimes we hate you.
Your batteries leak all over the place.
Your fumes make us ill,
So fork-lift truck stop your polluting,
Then we could all live together again.

Matthew Davis (11)
Great Wyrley High School

My Favourite Auntie

Pauline's not so much an aunt, more like a gran,
Only problem is I'm not eleven, but still in my pram.
Or so she thinks when she fusses a lot,
Never gives me treats and hugs - *not!*
Always moans at Uncle Brian, cousins Carl and Stu,
Never a cross word for me, that wouldn't do.
In a house that's full of men and boys,
My make-up and hairbrush are welcome toys.
She's small like my mum, but with ginger hair,
They both love me lots - quite a pair.
I've one or two aunts and I love them lots,
But of them all, *Pauline's the tops!*

Lisa Carroll (11)
Great Wyrley High School

New Year's Eve

In the dark winter sky the stars shine,
The local church bells begin to chime.
All the trees waving in the cold breeze,
As the midnight gardens start to freeze.
The snow flutters against my window-pane,
As the late-night revellers scuttle down the lane.
An owl begins to hoot
As the car horns begin to toot.
Happy New Year everyone!
Let's hope it will be an excellent one.

Chantelle Benton (11)
Great Wyrley High School

ME!

My name is Matt.
I'll hit you if you say I'm fat.
I love Holly my dog,
Even though she looks like a warthog.

I have a mum and a dad,
And a sister who is very mad.
I support Man United,
When they score I get excited.

The school I go to is called Great Wyrley,
In the mornings I have to get up very early.
Me and my mates hang around,
Mostly on the football ground.

Matthew Harper (11)
Great Wyrley High School

CHRISTMAS

C hurch bells ring, choirs sing
H ymns and praises to our King;
R oast turkey and trimmings on the plate,
I t's the 25th, an important date.
S nowflakes twirling to the ground,
    falling slowly without a sound;
T oys and gifts beneath the tree,
M erry children laugh with glee.
A busy day over, it goes so fast,
S anta goes home, he's finished at last.

Matthew Hibbs (12)
Great Wyrley High School

ALL ABOUT ME

My name is Andrew Jennings,
I live in Cheslyn Hay,
But it's for the Villa I would like to play.

I have a younger brother, Richard,
He is the pain of my life,
But my dad said that it can't be as bad
As having a wife.

My mum thinks I am such a dream,
It makes her want to shout and scream,
She just hopes over the next few years,
Great Wyrley High will help me buck up my ideas.

Andrew Jennings (11)
Great Wyrley High School

GOODBYE DIANA

Princess Di, you were really shy,
Now you've gone to live in the sky,
Away from the photos, the papers, the lies,
All the sadness has gone from your eyes.
You're with the angels and Dodi too,
But we all still love and miss you.

Your life was so full of vigour and zest,
You were very simply the best of the best,
So Princess Diana, we say goodbye and God bless.

Tara Pearce (11)
Great Wyrley High School

WHEN I STARTED SCHOOL

When I started school,
I felt a bit of a fool
Because my skirt blew up in front
Of all the boys.
I'm feeling more grown-up
As the days go by
And I'm throwing out my embarrassing old toys.

The first day I got lost.
It made me rather cross.
I felt silly when I arrived ten minutes late,
But the teacher didn't shout.
I soon found my way about
And now I think this school is great!

Hayley Myles-Blower (11)
Great Wyrley High School

BART SAYS

Eat a cow, man!
Eat my shorts, man!
Homer's really fat!
Lisa's smart, man!
But who cares about that?
Marge has long hair!
Even Maggie can fit in there!
Bart J (J for Jenius!) Simpson is cool
And that's a fact!
   Hey man!
Don't live in a caravan!

Gavinder Pawar (12)
Great Wyrley High School

A Box Of Dreams

A box beside my bed,
A heart-shaped box
Decorated with
Clouds and flowers.
I wake up
With lots of dreams in my head.
I put them in my box
Until night comes again,
And I open the box
And find more dreams to come true.

Jennika Patel (12)
Great Wyrley High School

An Exchange Between Walking And A Car!

I am better than you because . . .
I can run races
As well as make bases,
And I can ride a bike,
While you just reflect off the light.
With your pollution,
You make us ill.
I think we should return you with a bill.
Just because you're fast doesn't
mean you're best.
I always get the solution,
and you're there with the pollution.
At last I can hop
to the shop
While you have to wait in traffic.
Just because you can drive to Dover,
doesn't mean you can run us over.

Kelly Thompson (13)
Heathfield GM High School

BULLYING

I am always bullied for money,
I would give people a jar of honey,
If they would stop bullying me for money.
I would give them anything if I
could join them.
I would make a den, just for them,
I would do anything to go with them.
I would give anything to join them.
I wish they would stop bullying me
for money.
I would give them a jar of honey.
Please stop bullying me.
Please just leave me be.
Why me?
Why not him?
Please just stop bullying me!

Claire Graham (13)
Heathfield GM High School

LENNOX LEWIS

His jab is like lightning,
His punch is really strong,
His mind is all about fighting,
His guard is never wrong,
He flies like a butterfly,
He stings like a bee,
A bit like Mohammed Ali!

Shafeeq Mohammed (13)
Heathfield GM High School

ENGLAND V ITALY

E ngland play Italy away.
N ew boys want to play.
G lenn Hoddle wants to win.
L ive on the telly
A round the world.
N ext summer is the place to be.
D raw would get England through.

V ictory would do wonders.

I t would be a match of the play-offs
T erry Venables will be there.
A gainst one of the best teams in the world.
L ast chance to qualify.
Y oung boy's best dream.

In the end the score was . . .
    England 0 - Italy 0.

Jason Jeavons (13)
Heathfield GM High School

BULLIES

A teenage gang leader,
Who thought he knew it all,
Bossed and bullied other pupils,
Till they didn't want any more.

If you dare to disobey him,
He won't be very happy,
He will get a mate to bring you to him,
And do his dirty work.

Then after all you could be earless,
Or maybe fingerless,
So now you will be careful who you
Choose as friends.

So if you would, please spread the words,
So children won't end up in curbs,
Which would make our world much nicer
To live in.

Amy Butler (13)
Heathfield GM High School

THE CAT'S COLLAR

It was the ultimate pet collar
Boy was it worth a dollar
It was pointless spending that
Much on a cat
When all they do is sit on a mat.
The owner might have won the Lottery.
You could buy a piece of pottery.
The cat could be called Simon,
Because he had so many diamonds.
April is the cat's birthday,
And it could've been May.
You can't see the collar
15,000 is a lot of dollars.
It could be a wind-up.
She could've had a cup
It just goes to show
How potty people go.

Gemma Glasby (13)
Heathfield GM High School

AN EXCHANGE BETWEEN A LETTER AND A PHONE

Letter

You think you're so good with your ring,
But I do nearly the same thing.
You can repeat and repeat a letter,
But either way a phone is no better.
Phone calls have a high cost,
That's money you've lost.
So there, you say a phone is better,
      but really it's a letter!

Phone

All we have to do is pick up the phone,
While you don't speak to each other,
In any kind of tone.
I can spend as much time as I like
      on the phone with my friends.
But you, you're boring,
You don't have any kind of trends.
Go on, you try and say your part,
But you'll never ever beat my art!

Amy Blick (13)
Heathfield GM High School

ALCOHOL

Eighteen's the limit to drink
Some people don't stop and think.

Under-age drinking is against the law,
But people just shout out for more,
And more.

Some people have never tried it
Mums and Dads often buy it.

Some people get tipsy and
Some go dizzy.

People lie about on the streets
With nothing to say,
But the police come alone
And take you away.

Tara Arshad (13)
Heathfield GM High School

TIME FOR TUBBY BYE-BYES!

T he Teletubbies have been banned
E ven though they play in sand
L ack of English speech they say
E verybody thinks a different way
T he school still thinks they are doof!
U nderneath the school roof
B oys and girls say
B ut Miss, I'm gay
I don't want to play
E liot, the teacher says, go and stroke your cat
S he's a mean lady that teacher she looks like a rat!

Martyn Barnbrook (13)
Heathfield GM High School

TAUNTED TO SUICIDE

For such a long time she cried,
through the mental torment she tried.
To carry on again and again,
every day the same the same the same.

She lies awake at night,
filled with fear and fright.
Anticipating for the next day,
worrying what people might say.

For such a long time, she had to fight,
she had such will, such strength, such might.
One day she had taken enough stick,
from the cruel individuals taking the mick,
it had gone too far, the hurt was too much,
she kept quiet and made no fuss.
She had taken enough of the pain and strife,
she considered gas, and also a knife,
but alone with some pills she ended her life.

Michelle York (13)
Heathfield GM High School

BULLIES

Like I always say once a bully
always a bully.
They have done the damage,
they are surely on the rampage,
they cause pain, hatred, and much more,
victims are usually young and weak,
if you speak the future will look bleak.

Sean Tobin (13)
Heathfield GM High School

ALIENS

He came from outer space
The man with a massive face
With great big ears
And magnesium tears
The man with the massive face.

He had great big eyes
And told terrible lies,
The man with the great big eyes.

Yes! He had a head,
But it looked like a boiled egg.
The man with the egg-shaped head.

No! We're not alone,
Because they call me on the phone.
Their language is nothing but a clone
Oh! That drone upon the phone.

On the 25th September
An alien landed in Denver
Those lights on the 25th September.

The people say it was shaped like a saucepan,
Except with no exhausts man!
Oh that ship that's shaped like a saucepan
It landed at a place,
Where the big horses race
The place where the horses race.

Now I've shown you the face
And I've shown you the head
And now I'm off to bed.

Stuart Kettle (13)
Heathfield GM High School

THE DOCTOR WHO EVERYBODY RESPECTED

There was an old man from the City of Birmingham
Who was known as top doctor Billingham
He never gave anything to the poor
He was just a greedy, selfish, mean bore.
Many cupboards he had full of food
But never was in a giving mood.
He never spent a single penny
Unless it was really necessary.
He was a top doctor in medicine
Who killed people just for fun
By writing the wrong medicine.
He is very evil as you can see.
He was very famous in the city.
Why he was wicked was a big pity.
He was one of the best doctors around
Who was always evil bound.
Nobody ever seemed to realise
What evil thoughts went round his eyes.
The public respected him very much
They never knew he did such
Naughty things behind their back
Like a poisonous snake when it attacks.
He would finish people off one by one,
He never got caught for the things he'd done.
His figure was like a big fat greedy pig,
Whose appetite was very big.
He had many dear modified cars
Which were worth the price of ten pure gold bars.

Samina Begum (13)
Heathfield GM High School

AN EXCHANGE BETWEEN WATER AND FIRE

I put you out
Without a doubt.
I'm just the best.
I beat the rest.
No one can beat me
You are just like a helpless pea
You may say I drip all day
But you just melt things away
You're just a pest
Never give people a rest
You get on people's nerves
And send them up curves.

Rebecca Morgan (13)
Heathfield GM High School

SEVEN STAGES OF MAN

All the world's a stage,
And all the men and women merely players,
They have their exits and their entrances,
And one man in his time plays many parts,
His acts being seven ages.
At first, the baby is crying for its food.
Then the toddler, just starting school and making friends
And then the infant, learning and playing.
Then the junior kicking the ball and shouting.
Now the teenager makes new friends and has a laugh
The adult, all grown up, looks for a new life,
The old man is foolish and silly and all alone.

Andrew Worley (14)
Joseph Leckie School

SEVEN AGES OF MAN

All the world's a stage
The boy makes his entrance as a baby.
The baby cries for food and the baby sleeps.
Through the day, as the baby plays games, he giggles
The toddler tries to walk but fails each time by
Falling over. He starts to
Talk by saying names. He goes in a mood
Over anything. He wants people's attention
To play games. He is learning to speak properly
He does not like going to school so he
Pretends to be ill. At school he makes friends
But sometimes falls out. He starts to learn how
To read, and likes to play football. He becomes a manager
And starts to fall in love with girls. He is
An adult now and has chosen his life-time partner
To live with. He lives on his own, bored and
He will not listen to anyone else.

Jaswant Gill (13)
Joseph Leckie School

SEVEN STAGES OF MAN

All the world's a stage
And all men and women merely players.
They have their exits and their entrances.
First comes the baby when it's born crying and poohing.
And then the infant starts school, gradually learning
And then the teenager, turning into a young adult.
Then comes the adult trying to raise a family
And then comes a pensioner making his way to heaven.

Brijesh Maisuria (14)
Joseph Leckie School

SEVEN AGES OF MAN

All the world's a stage,
And all the men and women merely players.
They have their exits and their entrances.
And one man in his time plays many parts.
His act being seven ages.
At first the baby screaming and crying.
Then the toddler learning, to walk and to speak.
Then the infant starting school, upset and angry.
Then the junior, starting a new school.
Happy and chirpy to meet new friends.
Then comes the teenager mad and angry.
Shouting and screaming at friends and family.
Then the start of adult age, going to work.
Or to have a family first, then old age.
In retirement, hobbies become their life.

Seema Lal (13)
Joseph Leckie School

PRAYER BEFORE BIRTH

I am not yet born, please hear me.
Keep me away from all of the tigers and lions.
I am not yet born, please hear me.
So keep me comfortable and don't let me die.
I am not yet born, please hear me.
Please put all big nice green-leafed trees
and nice grass in our world.
I am not yet born, please hear me.
I wish to become an honest happy person.

Carl Hayes (11)
Joseph Leckie School

SEVEN AGES OF MAN

All the world's a stage.
And all the men and women merely players;
They have their exits and their entrances;
And one man in his time plays many parts,
His acts being seven ages.
First it's the baby crying and being sick,
Then learning how to crawl. Then the infant
Running around like a pest, and starting
Infant school. Then it is the junior,
Acting immature with shining bright eyes.
Then the worst, the teenager moaning and
Having mood swings, and looking for a lady
To love. Then the mature adult growing
A beard, and studying at school or uni.
Then becoming a father of a family,
Raising kids and looking after his wife.
And he has a wonderful job. Then, going
To collect his pension money because he
Has retired from his job. Now he is too
Old to work and rests at home because he
Cannot see that well, or he is not able to walk.

Randip Basra (13)
Joseph Leckie School

WARFARE

Amidst the anger and the hate,
Caught up in a nation of war.
Light up a candle of fate
And see the cold and the torn.

It is one's upbringing,
One's life, should we say.
But answer me one question . . .
Why no better suggestion?

Aarefa Mulla (14)
Joseph Leckie School

ALL THE WORLD'S A STAGE

All the world's a stage,
And all the men and women merely players,
They have their exits and their entrances,
And one man, in his time, plays many parts.
His acts being seven ages. At first the baby,
Comes into the world crying with hunger,
In the nurse's arms. Then the toddler comes
Along, starts his walking and tries to talk,
Then the infant ready to go to school,
With a happy face. Along comes the junior,
Boy with a satchel around his neck with,
A sad face, unwilling to go to school, then
The showing-off teenager doing her hairstyle,
Always showing off with her lover,
Then the adult, busy with her job,
A lady playing a part of mother,
Supporting her family with care,
Then comes the very hard stage of world,
The old-age pensioner is finishing his
Play. Coming to his exit and also,
Nearly dying. Has no teeth, no eyes,
And nothing else. Always shouting,
At others. Fighting among themselves.

Sophia Azam (13)
Joseph Leckie School

THE SEVEN AGES OF MAN

All the world's a stage,
And all the men and women
Merely players. They have their
Exits and their entrances
And one man in his time plays many parts
His acts being seven ages. At first the
Baby howling like a wolf in the night
The infant is very anxious
To read and write, on the verge of being an adult
Then a toddler screaming, parents refusing
To play games.
Then comes along a cheerful junior
Ready for his first day at school
Then he comes home
A moody grump full of guilt
As the parents
Get old, the toddler, junior then the grump
Leaves them and starts a life of his own.
As an old man he becomes helpless, needy
And lives his life over.

Amandeep Sambi (13)
Joseph Leckie School

PRAYER OF THE UNBORN CHILD

I am not yet born, please hear me
I would want all the tigers, cheetahs
and bumble bees away from me.

I am not yet born, please hear me
Keep me away from prison and drugs
and all sorts of bad things.

I am not yet born, please hear me
Please would you keep all the lovely
beautiful flowers, lovely fragrances,
and animals with me.

I am not yet born, please hear me
I would want to be a kind, honest,
gentle and loving person.

Zobea Raza (11)
Joseph Leckie School

THE SEVEN AGES OF MAN

The seven ages in your life
That play the part on the world's stage
Facing all life's lowly strife.
From cradle to grave, child to age.
Beginning with infant, crying all day.
For services, for attention, at his side you'll stay
The child's gain, the child's sorrow, the child's kicks and cries.
Woeful sinner, laughter and sadness, with daggers in his eyes.
The youth, the day-dreamer, jealous of fame.
The path of good omen, broken to maim.
The man of the house, mature and wise,
Knowing his place and far from demise.
The middle-ager, the worker the willing strong bear.
The well-fed forty-year-old, the lumberjack's axe,
He, the war-man, his past he'll share.
He, the chosen one to pay life's tax.
The old one, the crippled one, the sad and wiser man.
Won't accept help, won't accept thanks, doing all he can.
The decrepit, the elderly, taking his last breath
He falls to the ground, a new life in death.

Alan Williams (13)
Joseph Leckie School

ALL THE WORLD'S A STAGE

All the world's a stage,
And all the men and women merely players;
They have their exits and their entrances;
And one man in his time plays many parts.
His acts being seven ages.
At first the baby crying when he's born,
Sleeping when he's tired. Then the toddler,
Starting to walk, always falling,
Still at a crawl. Now the infant starting
School, making new friends. Then the junior
Starting a new school, starting to read and write,
Different words, different things.
Then the teenager becoming a man.
Started smoking, started taking drugs.
Now the adult who has got a family now,
He's more sensible, more careful now,
And last of all, a pensioner now,
Who starts losing his hair until he dies . . . !

Gavin Jukes (14)
Joseph Leckie School

PRAYER BEFORE BIRTH

I am not yet born
please protect me away
from the fierce tigers and
other wild animals.

I am not yet born
keep me away from dangers
and horrors of the spirit.

I am not yet born
I want to hear the birds singing
and I want the stars around me.

I am not yet born
I want to be a caring person
so I could be friends with people.

Gamal Idris (11)
Joseph Leckie School

SEVEN AGES OF MAN

All the world's a stage,
And all the men merely players.
They have their exits and their entrances;
And one man in his time plays many parts,
His acts being seven ages. At first,
The little baby in his mother's arms
Shouting and screaming:
Then the toddler fighting in the
Nursery play room over a toy.
Then the infant's first day at school
walking slowly and droopily to school
holding his mother's hand.
Then the junior going to junior school
on his own, but on the way calling for mates.
Then the senior who grows into a teenager
walking to school all big and tough and then
he gets to school and starts to play football with his mates.
Then the adult meets a girl. She becomes his wife,
They have two children, then the children start to grow up
And the two adults turn into two old aged pensioners
Who have to keep collecting their pensions
every month until they die . . . !

Ian Freeth (14)
Joseph Leckie School

SEVEN AGES OF MAN

All the world's a stage and all the men
and women merely players.
They have their exits and their entrances
and one man in his time plays many parts
his acts being seven ages.
At first he's born crying for hunger
for food or attention
and also puking all the time
and he is always needing to be changed and the
toddler is naughty all the time just for the sake of it
and always falling over because his balance is not yet
so steady and he now can feed himself
not like before, and then the small infant
and then he's a junior who's learnt and knows
right from wrong then a teenager.
Now he's an adult and has a lot of money from work
for his family and wife and then the OAP collecting
the pension from the Post Office getting wrinkly with loosening
teeth and then the pain and suffering of death.

Dipesh Patel (13)
Joseph Leckie School

PRAYER OF THE UNBORN CHILD

I am not yet born, please hear me.
Keep all dogs, snakes and rats away from me.
I want nothing like that near me.

I am not yet born, please hear me.
I wish never to be in danger
Or let no poison get to me.
Keep ghastly ghosts away from me.

I am not yet born, please hear me.
I'd like it if the tigers are there,
I still want the oceans still to be there,
I'd like to see the whales and dolphins swim and play.

I am not yet born, please hear me.
I want to be loved by everyone
And get on with everyone.
I want to be honest and kind,
But I am not born yet.

Rumi Choudury (11)
Joseph Leckie School

PRAYER BEFORE BIRTH

I am not yet born,
I'm very afraid of the barking dark,
the howling wolf,
of the frequent owl.

I am very afraid because I am not yet born.

The horrors of the world surround me
because I'm not yet born.
So hear me now people jabbing
and stabbing because I'm not yet born.

But I hope I am pleasant because
I hear singing and blooming all around
me because I am not yet born.

I am not yet born but soon I will
so keep my lovely flowers and trees
surrounding me in nature's bed.

Tanya Hayes (11)
Joseph Leckie School

SEVEN AGES OF MAN

All the world's a stage,
And all the men and women merely players,
They have their exits and their entrances;
And one man in his time plays his part.
His acts being seven ages.
At first the child cries like mad for,
Food in the nurse's arms.
Then the young schoolboy,
complains not to go to school,
Walking like a tortoise.
The young teenage boy,
In love, looking for a girl, goes out
in search for his only love, the young army soldier
is always doing his best, in the army.
He is always trying to keep a good name for himself.
The adult does his job quite well,
he has a big belly and,
he has a fake beard,
The sixth age of man is like a child,
He has a deep voice and acts strangely.
The old aged pensioner has no eyes,
no taste, no teeth. He has hardly anything.
He is dying slowly.

Asma Begum (13)
Joseph Leckie School

SEVEN AGES OF MAN

All the world's a stage.
And all the men and women
Merely players;
They have their exits and their entrances;
And one man in his time plays many parts,
His acts being seven ages.
At first a small, tiny boy awakens;
In the world feeling tired, lazy and helpless.
Moaning, groaning, crying in the lady's arms.
Then comes the lad, asking to marry her,
Being shy and doesn't know what to say.
Reading poems out to his love,
'Attention' says
The guard as he lifts his gun, ready to shoot.
A man going to court, frightened and scared,
doesn't know what to say.
A man looking very ordinary,
with glasses on his nose, and a pocket
on his side,
His big manly voice, turning again,
Towards childish bother.
Finally comes the old-age pensioner,
he has no teeth, no eyes.
No taste and most of all, he has nothing!

Hema Pandya (14)
Joseph Leckie School

ALL THE WORLD'S A STAGE

All the world's a stage
And all the men and women merely players.
They have their exits and their entrances.
And one man in his time plays many parts
His acts being seven ages.
At first the baby mewling and puking.
In his mother's arms crying and bawling,
Then comes the toddler learning to crawl.
Learning to speak, falling and standing up.
Then comes the infant starting school.
Carrying his school bag on his shoulder.
Running to school with a smile on his face.
Then comes the junior learning to read and write.
then comes the teenager with his mood swings,
And his bad habits and his boisterous ways.
Then comes the adult starting a family
Looking for a job and going to university.
And last of all comes the old-age pensioner who lost his taste.
And his eyesight almost gone with him.
Retired from work, going to rest in peace.

Kirendeep Attwal
Joseph Leckie School

PRAYER BEFORE BIRTH

I am not yet born, please hear me.
Please guard me from the tiger,
Lion and the blood-sucking bat.
Guard me from stabbing and killings.
Guard me from man-eating snakes.
Please protect me.

I am not yet born, please hear me.
Guard me from jail and mankind
bricking me in their walls.
I do not want the human race
to ruin my life.
Please save me from the horrors of the world.

I am not yet born, please hear me.
I'd like to hear the birds sing
in a morning, the trees dance
and the grass to say good morning.
Please help me to see and hear these things.

I am not yet born, please hear me.
I would like to read and write
dance and sing and be honest
and trustworthy.
Please help me and guard me.

Please hear me.

Emma McDonald (11)
Joseph Leckie School

ALL THE WORLD'S A STAGE

All the world's a stage,
And all men and women merely players,
They have their exits and their entrances,
And one man in his time plays many parts,
His acts being many ages. At first is the
baby crying for food. Then comes the
toddler playing at school with Plasticine.
Next comes the teenager getting dressed up
to go to a disco. Fourthly comes the
young adult looking for a job. Then
comes the middle age, getting up early to
go to work. Then comes the man getting old,
travelling towards his exit, he is getting
back to being a child ready to die.

Rumela Begum (13)
Joseph Leckie School

THE POND

The pond shimmers in the moonlight,
With only the movement of ripples.
The leaves rustle in the wind,
It is peaceful unlike the morning
Which is soon to come.

The sun peeps over the horizon,
Throwing rays of sunlight here and there.
The silence is disturbed when the ducks awake,
For they splash in and out of the water.

This is the pond.

Joanna Sidhu (11)
Saint Martin's School for Girls

ICY MORNING

The frost is crisp upon the ground,
And ice is on the pond, strong and proud.
The sun appears, the ice disappears,
And all that is left is the chill
Of the night.

The reeds stand high and tall
Like watching ladies,
Heads bent at the end.
The lilies are covered in shining white snow,
Hiding their crinkled brown petals
And their leaves are as soft as soft can be,
Floating away as if they were free,

Kate Stone (11)
Saint Martin's School for Girls

IN AND AROUND THE POND

The water is shallow,
Shallow as the eye can see,
The green, green grass
Swaying happily, merrily.

The smooth rippling water,
It ripples in the sun,
The ducks dipping in and out,
Having lots of fun!

Five little ducklings dipping in and out,
Down swooped a magpie,
And tried to fish one out.

Sophie Gibson (11)
Saint Martin's School for Girls

The Quad

A place for all seasons tucked silently away
Giving solitude by night and peace by day
Where four stout walls in their quest never fail
To protect from the freezing frenzy of the cruel winter gale
Or harness the sunshine on a warm summer's day
Or the intoxicating aroma of the scented petals of May
Day unfolded after day, hot and tranquil under skies blue and cool
Faithfully reflecting in the mirror glass pool
Where ducks take refuge from the world outside
And darting dragonflies dip and glide
The lush velvet carpet lies quietly in wait
For strolling and thinking of future and fate
Or silently meditating on things that have past
Life's ever-changing pattern and things that don't last
Of beautiful memories of days full of mirth
And this celestial place which is still on our earth.

Rebecca Dudill (12)
Saint Martin's School for Girls

The Quad

Hedges grow and brambles lie on the floor,
The pond lies still,
The ducks dive in and out of the water,
Swimming gracefully,
Nothing disturbs the quad.

Birds fly in and out of the trees,
All is silent except the songs of
the birds and the hum of the bees,
Beauty lies waiting for all to see.

Amy Walton (11)
Saint Martin's School for Girls

THE POND

As the ducks paddle around
The green smelly water,
The fish underneath glow through the mirror.
The children sit and watch leaning too far over.
Splash! Guess what's happened,
Laughter echoes around.
The ducks spring up and down
With the force of the ripples.
A mass dripping clambers to the edge.
Smelling and ponging with black
Mud sticking to all parts.
'Just wait till you get home'
Laughed his friend.
His friend said, 'I don't want to go home now.'

Joanna McDonagh (11)
Saint Martin's School for Girls

THE DUCKS

In the quad the ducks play in the pond,
swimming in and out of the water lilies.
The smallest always last.

When they want food, the ducks look
around the place very thoroughly.

When the ducks have finished their
food they play in the water again.
Whenever people look at them swimming
through the lilies, they don't appear to be disturbed.
They don't even look up.
That is the ducks' behaviour.

Ailish Cotter (11)
Saint Martin's School for Girls

The Quad

At the quad I sit each day,
Listening to the birds chirp away.

When the birds want bread they'll come and beg,
And then go when they're well fed.

In the bush they sometimes rush
When people come and have a look.

In the pond the ducks sometimes play
Sun, cloud, rain or all the day.

As the wildlife come out
The fish they scatter all about.

In the sparkling water the ducks dive and play.
At the pond it glistens each day.

Late at night the frogs come out to see
If there is food about.

Then the ducks go in to rest
And go to sleep in their nest.

Amy Smith (11)
Saint Martin's School for Girls

The Quad

The evening sun shone down on the quad,
Gently lighting it up with golden beams,
The dew on the grass shimmered in the light,
And the pond was silent and calm.

The deep emerald green lily pads,
Stretched out like umbrellas over the pond,
Looking shiny as if they had just been polished,
Ready for their flowers to arrive in spring.

The silence of the quad was only broken,
By the continual sound made by the ducks,
As they finished their evening meal,
And prepared to go to bed.

As darkness fell over the quad,
Like a black velvet curtain falling into place,
The noises all died away,
As the world settled down to sleep.

Lucy Archer (11)
Saint Martin's School for Girls

MOONLIGHT ON THE POND

The moon sparkled in the sky casting a golden glow
against the ocean blue pond.
The wind blew against the tall handsome grass making
it sway gently to and fro.
The stars sparkled like jewels, each one a perfect diamond.
The air was clear but yet smelt of red, ripe roses at their
fullest bloom.
Ripples appeared on the pond, showing the age of so
many wonderful years, each one showing more beauty than ever.
The lilies bobbed on the water so delicately, no one dared
touch one for it looked so fragile and would shatter into
a thousand pieces.
The water looked like glass catching the moon just at
the right moment, then shining at its very brightest,
showing the world what power and grace it had.
Those glorious hours of beauty at its fullest,
then disappearing for a golden sunrise.
But be sure that the moon awaits.

Kate Pomeroy (11)
Saint Martin's School for Girls

THE GARDEN

It's a warm summer's day
As I sit on the grass.
Then suddenly something comes in my way
It's the little ducklings passing.
They look so sweet as they play,
They are playing and running fast.

As I sit I feel a breeze.
I looked around
And saw the trees
And on the trees I found a sparrow.

As the sparrow went out of sight
I admired the flowers colourfully bright,
Red, orange, yellow and blue.
Fresh smells of the morning dew.

Christine George (11)
Saint Martin's School for Girls

THE QUAD

Within the school a quad is to be found,
Planted with shrubs and bushes,
New flowers will soon be planted,
To offer colour to gaze upon,
A bird table and a pond
Give wildlife a place to call home,
New ducklings have come to live,
Giving me a delightful scene.

Jenny Pallett (11)
Saint Martin's School for Girls

THE QUAD

In our school quad there are some ducks,
Who love to paddle round.
Sometimes they swim on their backs,
Or maybe they play around.

The pond has lovely lilies
That are very pretty too.
It is a lovely sight,
When there is morning dew.

The mother duck was very proud,
Until she flew away.
Now the ducks are left alone,
We'll feed them every day.

Victoria Lucas (12)
Saint Martin's School for Girls

OUR GARDEN

Safely encased within walls of brick,
Bushes rise up quite tall and thick.
In this little place of peace,
The wonders of nature will never cease.

A single tree rises straight and tall,
Right in the centre to be marvelled by all.
Next to this lies a calm little pond,
Of which, I know, I have grown quite fond.

Slowly, the ripples roll gently by,
Colliding with lilies that on the surface lie.
The season is changing, we're nearing the Fall,
Next year the garden will be reborn once more.

Samantha Greenfield (11)
Saint Martin's School for Girls

MOONLIT MIRROR POND

Crystal clear water
Mysteriously moonlit by silver beams.
Calm and gently rippling
In the airy night-time breeze.
Tall green reeds
Rustle and whisper as they sway.
Stately lily pads,
Like kings and queens
With crown-like petals of delicate pink,
Float proudly on the mirror-like water,
The radiant surface,
Sprinkled with silver,
Conceals the unseen world beneath.

Ruth Ainsworth (12)
Saint Martin's School for Girls

THE POND

In the middle of the quad,
There lies a quaint pond.
It's home to the lilies, rushes and ducklings,
And sparkles and glints in the pleasant warm sun.
The pond is still until the wind sends a ripple,
Or when the ducklings come in for a splash and a paddle.
The rushes grow tall and swing to the breeze,
And then there's the lilies that float gently with ease.
The quad's a happy place,
As long as it's kept clean and safe!

Ciara Phillips (11)
Saint Martin's School for Girls

THE POND

They look into the murky water,
They hear the monster,
But they don't care,
They want to play.

Slash, splosh, slish, splish, splash,
There go the five little ducks,
Under the water,
Eating all the algae.

The giant lily pads get in their way,
The long lacy trees lean over them,
The sun goes in
And the monster comes back.

Quack, mummy's back,
It's time to go to sleep.
They wrap up warm and go to bed,
And think about the day ahead.

Lucinda Manning-Brown (11)
Saint Martin's School for Girls

GOD

Is he real?
Is he there?
Is he a ball of fire?
Or a cloud of air?

Is he a star?
Is he a leaf?
Is he a fish?
Or a coral reef?

Is he slim?
Is he tall?
Is he fat?
Or a guardian for us all?

Is the world ours?
Is it his?
Is he war?
Or is he peace?

Is he a he?
Is he a she?
I don't know,
but I believe!

I believe in him,
He *is* there,
He is love,
He is care.

Bhinder Chopra (17)
St Thomas More RC Comprehensive School

HOMELESS

I'm left on the street with nothing to eat.
I have got cold feet and nowhere to stay.
I just sit on the street and sleep all day.
I beg and I beg but no one will help.
They just walk past all by themselves.
I try to sing to get some money
But everyone laughs and thinks I'm funny.
I cry all day to get some money and
Some people just give me a penny.
I laugh at them and give it them back.
Sometimes someone might give me a fag
Or a drag of a fag.
The nasty kids that go past
They take the micky and then run off.
They tease me when I have a fag
Because I am such a tramp.
I walk around the streets to find something to eat
But all there is, is mouldy bread.
I try not to eat it but I have to get something to eat.
I cannot even find a drink.
One of these days I am going to get dehydrated
And go to hospital.
Then I will ask them to kill me
Because I have nowhere to stay.
They might clean me up and put me in a home
And buy me some clothes.
At least I won't be on the street alone.

Emma Holland (14)
Selly Oak Special School

HOMELESS

I am a tramp
With no money or home
I sit on the street with nothing to eat
I shout out 'Money' but nobody cares
I wish I was dead
That will teach them to spare
The kind of money I could share
I wish I could think of a better way to live
But all I can do is sit on the street
I try to eat food which is dirty and cold
But people walk by with not a care in the world
People look at me and think what a tramp
I hope I don't live on the streets forever
Even if I did people would not care
Think what it would be like if you were like me
Then you would care
Some people are lucky and have a home to go to
All I have is a cardboard box
I struggle through the day and smile my best
Hoping one day to be like the rest.

Rebecca Griffin (15)
Selly Oak Special School

HOMELESS

You can't imagine what it is like
To be a poor person having to fight for
your life.
Starving with hunger but no one cares.
Trying to understand that no one will be
there.
The cruel human race just laughs in my
face.
But one day my luck might change.
Then I will be laughing at them.
Then they might understand what
homelessness is like.

Anthony Boyce (15)
Selly Oak Special School

THOUGHTS OF A HOMELESS PERSON

I was brought up on the street
Without anything to eat.
I have been here for years now,
It feels like I am dying slowly.
No one says hello to me.
I am used to it all now.
It doesn't bother me.

Michael Edwards (14)
Selly Oak Special School

I'M HELD SPELLBOUND BY FOOTBALL

When I go to Coventry City,
I cast a spell so they can win.
But then the football blows up.
The referee buys a new ball.
The ball broke into bit,
The referee had no money.

Joseph Gilbey
Sherbourne Fields School

THE WORST WITCH

I'm the worst witch.
I turned Danny into a granny.
I'm the worst witch.
I turned a frog into a pog.
I even turned a phone into a pine cone,
so please leave me alone.

Max Garelick (10)
Sherbourne Fields School

HALLOWE'EN

Mum, make a pumpkin pie
Bats fly high in the sky.

Ghosts and witches come to the door
Asking for tricks and treats galore.

Then we have scary stories in the dark
Then I heard a wolf scratching on the bark of a tree.
All my dreams that night frightened me.

Emma Barnes (11)
Sherbourne Fields School

THE MAGIC BOX

I had a box and it was magic
I went inside and it was like I was playing
Football!
Then my Dad took me out
And I wanted to go back in and,
I did!
It was dark.
Then I was playing in . . .
The World Final Football Cup of the Year.

Gagandeep Dogra (10)
Sherbourne Fields School

SPELL

Candle magic,
My candle magic.
My candle magics
Animals from the jungle and
Take-aways from India
Friends from different countries and
Takes me back in time.
I can be invisible.
I'm spellbound!

John Lawlor (11)
Sherbourne Fields School

Spot Kick

A man is now walking down the tunnel of his dreams,
The crowd start to shout at the two teams.
As the whistle blows friendship is put aside,
It's time for Birmingham to kill this Barnsley side.

A defender comes off, a striker comes on,
It's the Israelite Alon Mizaron,
He passes to the man who calls,
As Tinkler tackles, the man falls.

The tackler sees red and Blues win a free kick,
The ball is passed to the man from a sharp flick.
He fires the ball like a bullet from a gun,
The power starts to intimidate everyone.

The shot is impossible for the goalie to get,
And the ball hits the back of the net.
The goal that was scored was a scorcher,
For Barnsley, this is torture.

As the second half gets underway,
People are glad they came, even if they had to pay.
Alon Mizaron is in the box,
He is fouled by their new player Ruel Fox.

Fox's temper has gone to his head showing his ethic's poor,
The ref shows his authority and shows him the door.
The man places the ball on the spot,
He is now starting to get hot.

Before he takes it he decides to spit,
Now he starts his run for the spot kick.
Just before he kicks the ball,
He collapses flat on the floor.

His heart had given it one last smack,
He collapsed and died of a heart attack.

Ian Smith (13)
Solihull School

WIND

Drifting through the leaves as she passes by,
Giving an invisible coolness,
The mysterious gas may contain the speck of dust,
But could be like a doctor on a hot summer's day.

She loops around us,
Helping country by country,
For their windmills and power stations.
Sailors have also been her close friend.

But is she really a good friend,
People losing homes and getting too cold.
The fallen trees and flowers,
All have been an enemy to her.

Moving on year by year,
She has flown further into the distance,
Machine and fuel,
Have meant she can go back into her own world.

An old friend,
Now has turned into a strong enemy.

Yitao Duan (13)
Solihull School

Penalty

The crowd entered like bees around honey,
Singing and chanting various songs,
We kicked off and had most of the possession,
The ball yo-yoing up and down the pitch.

The deadlock was eventually broken,
When a high looping ball fell to their striker's feet,
He zigzagged along the pitch,
Until he hit a curving shot into the top left corner.

The equaliser came quickly,
From the corner a super hard-hitting header,
Beating everyone including the diving goalkeeper,
The final whistle was about to go,

When Bill Bobings was brought down,
In the penalty area,
The referee pointed to the spot,
The die was cast, a penalty.

The sweat dripped from my head
Like rain from a broken gutter,
The goal looked tiny,
I was a million miles away,
As I ran up, I struck a perfect shot.

G-o-o-o-o-a-a-a-a-l-l-l-l!
The ecstasy was immense,
I had scored in a Cup Final,
Success was sweet.

Will Hudson (13)
Solihull School

Death Fish

He glides through the water,
Like a bird through air,
More fearsome than a lion,
Stronger than a bear.

Land is his boundary,
Sea, his domain,
No one can stop him,
So we let him reign.

His jaw of daggers,
Is stained with death,
And his stomach is full,
With raw bones and flesh.

He lurks in the shadows,
Of caverns and dreams,
Dressed in death,
His eyes like beams.

He preys on fear,
And minds and dreams,
He is the great predator,
Of the seven seas.

He cares not for fear,
And he needs no sight,
For his vision can cut,
The water like a knife.

To him we are prey,
Like a fish or a seal,
We are nothing big,
Just one other meal.

John Swani (13)
Solihull School

THE SWEET SHOP

The clock strikes half-past three,
The sweet shop's door opens,
The shopkeeper's grin widens,
As the little children run.

The children's eyes sparkle,
As rows of jars unfold,
Delicious nibbles for children,
Which covers their teeth in mould.

Rhubarb and custard, or liquorice,
A delicacy for some,
Or an appetising bar of chocolate,
Or nibble on a tasty iced bun.

The essence of herbal tablets,
The sweet scent of Devon toffee,
Inhale this fragrance of magic,
It's more addictive than a cup of coffee!

The little children squeal in bliss,
As the shopkeeper's till gets warm,
A thousand little piglets grunt
Their greedy famished demands.

The time wears on, they begin to leave,
Like a flock of heedless sheep,
Devouring helpless chocolate bars,
Knocking back sherbet neat!

He closes the door behind them,
And looks at his loot in glee,
Knowing they'll be back tomorrow,
At the time half-past three!

Oliver Manning-Brown (13)
Solihull School

ADVANCE FROM THE TRENCH

Shells and bullets over my head,
my boots feel as if they are lead.
The bodies increase and people burn,
why don't they just tell us to return?

All this waste of life and limb,
and for what, is our future dim?
The sight, sound and smell,
they all increase with every shell.

The world slows down and seems to stop,
all you hear are those who drop.
The cries and screams ring about,
I just want to yell out.

As the enemy gets in sight,
the whites of their eyes fills me with fright.
Words cannot describe the fear of death,
every second could be your last breath.

I look up and see the aim,
then all I feel is surging pain.
The aim is defended,
my life, has it ended?

Mark Askew (13)
Solihull School

EAGLE

He soars high,
His wings spread wide,
The gold-plated feathers glimmering in the morning air,
His beak with its menacing curve,
Eyes fiery like black diamonds,
Claws devilishly sharp,
He swoops,
Soars,
Spots his prey
The wings twist with brilliant elegance,
He drops like a stone,
As silent as the wind he swoops,
The mouse,
A smell of fear lingering in the air,
The eagle swipes with pinpoint accuracy,
Dragging the mouse high into the air,
Back to the nest,
Breakfast is served.

Richard Howell (13)
Solihull School

CAR RANGE

Fast and red
Big and powerful
Small and sporty
Slim and streamlined.

Ferraris or Fiats
Porsches or Peugeots
Lamborghinis or Ladas
It doesn't matter what
You drive they all do
The same job.

Posers drive Porsches
Rich people Rolls Royces
Families drive Fords
Teachers drive Toyotas
And sixth-formers drive *fast.*

Fred Hopkins (13)
Solihull School

PEACE AT LAST!

The sunlight was dancing on the rippling water,
Two lovers, gazing, romantically into each other's eyes,
Oblivious of everything except each other,
Flash went the paparazzi!

In the glamorous surroundings of the Paris Ritz,
Hidden from view an intimate meal,
Love tokens of a blossoming relationship exchanged,
Only caught by the prying eye of a security camera,
Flash went the paparazzi!

Stars twinkling like diamonds in the Paris night-sky,
Minds filled with dreams of a wonderful cruise,
Thoughts of a joyful family reunion,
Flash went the paparazzi!

The night seemed so dark,
The tunnel-mouth loomed like a cavern before them,
A bang, a crash, a deafening silence,
Flash went the paparazzi!

The intoxicating smell from a sea of flowers,
The overwhelming grief of a broken nation,
Peace at last,
Flash went the paparazzi!

Christopher Edwards (13)
Solihull School

FACING FIRE

A pyramid of wood and paper
Waiting to be lit.
The match was struck,
Then soon the fire was roaring.

We sat around on logs and planks,
Talking in the fading evening light.
The fire started to die down
So more wood, hessian and fuel.

When suddenly the hellish flames
Found the dreaded fuel -
The fire erupted, blowing out ash!
The smouldering ash struck my face.

A quarter inch from my eye
Burning through my skin!
I jumped up screaming, clutching my face.
I ran inside feeling blindly for a cold flannel.

Mum panicked, sprayed antiseptic,
Just missing my precious eye,
But the pain continued.
We sped home, uneasy silence loud inside the car.

A lecture from an angry doctor on the danger of fire.
Daily visits from District Nurse to dress the wound.
She did a good job -
Lucky not to be scarred, lucky not to be blind!

James Clarke (13)
Solihull School

THE SIMPSONS

Homer Simpson,
Chubby and bald.
Fatso is what he may often be called.

Bart Simpson,
The spiky haired devil,
Could also be called 'The World's Greatest Rebel'.

Lisa Simpson,
Little Miss Sweet,
Fellow pupils in tests will often be beat.

Marge Simpson,
With hair four feet tall,
Keeps the house clean from wall to wall.

Maggie Simpson,
Just sucks on her dummy,
Would be lost without hugs from her mummy.

The Simpsons could be the family from hell,
With life just a huge roller-coaster.
With crazy adventures week after week,
Humour engulfs their show.

David Massey (13)
Solihull School

IF ONLY I COULD BE...

If only I could be
Like a plant or a tree,
And be able to see
And watch over thee.

If only I could be
As free as a bee,
Black and yellow
But unable to harm thee.

If only I could be
Just like the sea,
But not be able to see
The pollution dumped in by thee.

If only you could agree
That being a human being,
Does not give us the right
To do things for free.

Let's not destroy the tree,
Let's not harm the bee,
Let's not pollute the sea,
But let us all agree
This shall become a world for future of thee!

Richard Bower (13)
Solihull School

Snow

Blanketing the cars and covering the garden,
The snow had come during the night.
The sun glistened on the fallen snow,
But clouds were now eclipsing the sun.

Then shrieking broke the peaceful tranquillity,
As children poured out of the houses,
Their faces shining with glee,
The snowman construction begins and the snowballs are fired.

Little snowflakes are now falling constantly,
The mothers call in their children.
A blizzard has been forecast,
As peace is now restored.

The snow is now pelting down,
With it hail is bouncing off the ground.
Only the brave would be on the road,
But the short spell doesn't last long.

The footprints have now gone,
But the powder is melting and rain is looming,
The snow is disappearing but fixed in my mind,
Are the diamonds encrusted on the trees.

Gurinder Sunner (13)
Solihull School

THE SEA

As I see the waves crash on the rocks below,
I see what the sea can do.
The waves look menacing as they roll
in from a distant sea.
I hear the seagulls scream in distant echoes,
as the dark clouds blanket the sea.

A rush of tide passes over the rocks beyond,
spelling danger to those who dare trespass its field.
Crash!
As the lightning strikes the sea is engulfed with light
which then fades into the dark blue shadows.

The wind strengthens and pushes the sea outward
as the downward wind makes spray upon the rolling sea.
The sea is controlled by the weather
and nothing else is in command.

Alex Homer (13)
Solihull School

MELLOW YELLOW

I own a little yellow Mini,
Which I really love and treasure,
People say it's old and tinny,
But driving it's a pleasure!

Cruising down the open road,
Sunlight dancing on the bonnet,
The road ribbons around many bends,
For my little yellow comet.

It may not be any E-Type Jag,
Or even a Mercedes-Benz,
But I love my little automobile,
And the colour's just the best!

Although my car is really great,
It's getting old and frail,
And soon it'll be going to that 'great garage in the sky',
But leaving behind a blazing trail!

Tom Osborne (14)
Solihull School

THE QUEEN OF THE RESIDENCE

She wandered in, slowly, elegantly,
Her sleek, coat and graceful walk,
Outdone only by her vanity and superiority.

She glided calmly about the room,
And seemed to float effortlessly
Over even the toughest of obstacles.

She turned to me and marched over
In my direction, and looked down at
Me from below, with eyes that

Could only belong to a goddess.
Yet if you looked through these sharp,
Beautiful eyes, it was clearly simple

That you would find such warmth
And compassion to last eternity,
However hard she tried to hide it.

Tom Willshaw (13)
Solihull School

THE CACTUS

The cactus fights on,
Losing to the fiery foe.
He crouches up small,
To minimise the pain of the attack.

The cactus shrivels up,
Ready to go to his dry, sandy grave.
It is all over, the sun has won . . .
Or has it?

Something falls on him.
It is cool and refreshing.
The storm relieves the roasting heat.
Life pours into him, he grows.

Offspring appear,
Draining his energy,
But with the recent rain,
He survives.

He grows proud as he sees
A ring of children,
Sitting round him
In an orderly row.

He grows old and weak.
He waits for his coming fate.
More rains are coming,
But not soon enough.

His children do not mourn.
They concentrate on survival.
Their father went through so much,
Yet is not remembered.

Robert Scott (13)
Solihull School

How Unlucky

It was a bright spring morning,
And the sun burst through the clouds.
It smashed on the early morning dew,
Bounced into my eyes and dazzled me.
It hadn't been a good week.
I had fallen down the stairs,
And crashed my brand new sparkling Mini
All this had happened since I walked under a ladder,
And let a black cat cross my path.
Today I was meeting my friend and his son in the park.
Whilst riding there I hit a lamppost.
I had to walk with a bent bike for the rest of the way.
His son had a kite,
A huge metallic blue kite with a fifteen foot long tail.
I had to have a go at hurling its glistening body
High in the sky and swooping like a soaring eagle.
I set off running faster and faster.
As I ran the string attached itself to me,
In my *trouser zipper*.
The string and wind held strong,
And the resisting kite refused to come down.
As I pulled,
'Ahhhhhh!'
They ripped clean away and flew off with the kite,
I made a run for my wonky bike.
I set off wobbling like a penguin on stilts.
'He lost my kite Daddy, *waaahhh!*' wailed the boy.
I don't think I'll go out tomorrow,
It's too much of a risk!

Jonathan Thorne (13)
Solihull School

STORM AT SEA

With a blinding flash,
And a deafening crash,
The heavens parted,
And came down upon us.

The waves rise and fall,
Until they make a solid wall,
The murky water fell,
And came down upon us.

The sail flapped like a furious flag,
It ripped on a spiky crag,
The white fabric enveloped the sky,
And came down upon us.

Choppier and choppier the sea became,
Our faces whipped by the lashing rain,
The undercurrents ran riot,
And smashed up through us.

Clinging tightly onto the floating wood,
Thinking of the times of good,
The cold wrapped us like a cloak,
And we were no more.

Jamie Partington (13)
Solihull School

MY BLACK COUNTRY BALLAD - THE DAY TRIP

We day 'ave no 'olidays,
Cos we day 'ave no money
So we went out with the Sunday School,
And Mother gid us bread and honey.

We allus went to the sayside,
And spent a penny on some rock,
Yo ad to share with your mates,
Then we ran down to the dock.

The weather was allus 'ot,
And we all went paddlin in the say,
We day 'ave no buckets and spades,
But that never spoiled our play.

When we had to 'goo 'omm,
Everyone felt sad,
But the teachers bless'em,
Gid all the kids a brown bag.

The bag had lots of goodies,
Liquorice, an orange and sherbert dip,
What bliss we thought as 'omm we went,
To dream of next year's trip.

Oh what a time we had,
We day 'arf have a lof,
All sitting on the sharra bang,
We never wanted to ger off.

Adam Lester (13)
Summerhill School

Diana

I heard there was a crash,
not to know it was Di,
I found out with a dash,
Oh Di we really love you.

The car was at a speed,
to kill the most precious.
So we say kill our speed.
Oh Di we really love you.

One-twenty was the speed,
curling, swirling around.
Crash, bang then the greed.
Oh Di we really love you.

There once was a lady,
who cared for everyone.
It helped a girl called Monday
Oh Di we really love you.

Harry is the youngest
Willy helps him along,
Charles is the greatest.
Oh Di we really love you.

Diana wore smart clothes
pound and pound it won't matter
because we still love her.
Oh Di we really love you.

Sam Robbins (13)
Summerhill School

THE BALLAD OF DEATH

Losing someone special
makes you feel alone.
You think the next life taken
may just well be your own.

Something is upsetting you
it only happened today.
Someone very close to you
unfortunately passed away.

For you and other people
death means only pain.
It's an upsetting tragic loss
and definitely is no gain.

Someone who's been there for you
and helped you sort things out
may not always be there
of that there is no doubt.

The pain is ruthless, there is no cure
although all this is in your head.
You're scared, alone and feeling depressed
and all because that someone is dead.

In all the times you've needed help
for you their hand they lend.
But now you cannot pay them back
because it is the end.

Natalie Jones (12)
Summerhill School

THE HOLIDAY JOURNEY

Running for the bathroom,
Tripping down the stairs,
Sprinting through the kitchen,
Falling over the chairs.

Mom gets out the cereal,
Pouring on the milk,
I don't want those Frosties,
And I want hot milk.

Grabbing for the suitcase,
Mom runs to the door,
Have you got the sun cream dear,
Oh no! It's on the floor.

Looking for the teddy bear,
I left it over there,
You'll have to go without it
Dear, we're going to be so late,
The man at the holiday will
Be shutting up the gate.

Grabbing two or three pillows,
And a sleeping bag,
Looking for the socks and shoes,
And the fashion mag.

Changing that flat tyre,
Putting up the roof rack,
Fitting on the suitcase,
Throwing in the back-sack.

Just about ready to go,
Sally screams, 'Oh no! Oh no!'
Finally they set off,
Shutting up the gate,
Ready for the six hour journey,
Off to meet Sally's mate.

Melissa Doody (12)
Summerhill School

THE SEASONS IN THE YEAR

Spring is the first season in the year,
When flowers begin to grow,
And little sheep come out to play,
And the sun starts to show.

Summer is the second season,
The nice weather is here to stay,
The sun is shining in the sky,
And I can go out to play.

Autumn is the third season,
The leaves begin to fall,
The days are getting shorter,
As winter comes to call.

Winter is the fourth season,
And Christmas is getting near,
The days are getting colder,
As we start another year.

The seasons come and the seasons go,
As another year goes by,
Winter lasts forever,
But summer seems to fly.

Kate Hamer (12)
Summerhill School

QUEEN OF HEARTS

The world woke up one Sunday morning,
Thought it was another day,
And went to turn the TV on.
It wasn't another normal day.

All the headlines spread with sadness,
The woman who was helpful and gay,
Died in France 'cause of paparazzi.
It wasn't another normal day.

People travel to give their tributes,
To the Queen of our Hearts every day,
She helped the people who were left alone.
It wasn't another normal day.

Everyone's thoughts, sympathy and sadness,
Reflects on her sons William and Harry,
Who went to church the day she died.
It wasn't another normal day.

One whole week has come and passed,
Everyone has something they want to say,
The letters and flowers show our love,
It wasn't another normal day.

The gun carriage held our Princess,
The flowers were thrown along the way,
So many people said 'Goodbye'.
It wasn't another normal day.

> Everywhere came to a grieving standstill,
> People lined the motorway,
> The driver removed a bundle of flowers.
> It wasn't another normal day.
>
> All the world honoured Diana.
> It wasn't another normal day.

Frances Bennett (12)
Summerhill School

PRINCESS DIANA

In front of the telly we all sat one August morning
We'll never forget the look of the shock upon our face
Gone without a trace.

Princess Diana was wonderful
She helped in every way
She helped millions and thousands
She helped without pay.

Her proud sons are William and Harry
They loved her very dearly
You could see this quite clearly.

This was a tragedy the way that this had happened
Well what can we say
We loved her very dearly in each and every way.

Through the good times and the bad times
Come what may, she was always there
At the end of the day.

And now it makes everyone feel so sad
We are glad
That Diana did not die sad.

Zoe Riley (12)
Summerhill School

A Ballad On Trains

From the station down the track
clickerty clack down the track.
Over bridges, under bridges, down the track
clickerty clack, clickerty clack.

Through the cities, towns and villages,
down the track, clickerty clack,
up and over hills and streams.
Through the woods the train
will go down the track clickerty clack.

To the seaside trains will go
down and up the track.
See a train go whizzing by
and hear its whistle blow.

Karl Oakley (12)
Summerhill School

Why Me?

I get up in the morning
Don't want to go to school
Because I am afraid
Of looking like a fool.

I tried to be friendly
As friendly as I can
They just stopped and looked at me
What a fool I am.

Everybody keeps ignoring me
I do the best I can
They giggle and point
I feel they don't give a damn.

I don't know who to talk to.
I don't know what to say.
I don't know if you'll believe me
And tell me to go away.

Why do they keep picking on me?
What is it I have done?
I want to make things better
And make it lots of fun.

Jane Cutler (12)
Summerhill School

CHOCOLATE

It soothes your throat totally as it goes down
It's so lovely you won't ever frown
Galaxy and Dairy Milk are the best
To enjoy them you need to take a rest
We know chocolate is not good
But you hear a voice saying you should
It's brown it's nice it's very tasty
It doesn't taste nice when it's pastry
Cakes and biscuits are covered with it
Wouldn't you just love to be in a chocolate pit.
They say eating chocolate will give you spots
But I don't care, I love chocolate drops.
So if you're on a diet and don't want to stop
Don't sneak to get some chocolate from the corner shop.

Callum Bradley (12)
Summerhill School

OIL

Early in the morning,
The tanker engine roared,
The harbour doors opened,
And down the rain poured.

Out the tanker went carrying oil and all,
The water roared up,
And covered the men, pushing them to a fall.

The tanker rolled over,
Not once but twice,
The big tanker bent,
When it hit the water, that felt like ice.

The tanker creaked,
As it swirled,
It looked like a snowstorm,
When it curled and twirled.

The side buckled, and was nearly bent,
The men called for help,
As the floor started to dent.

The oil barrels opened,
And in the sea they fell,
The men tried to catch them but did not succeed,
The fish and birds weeped and started to yell.

As the barrels floated,
The oil was to spread,
The creatures swam,
But the oil covered their heads.

The men secured the others,
Then had a rest,
They waited for help to come,
As they had all done their best.

Danny Thurley (12)
Summerhill School

BETRAYAL

Trust is felt in friendships,
Long and lasting love,
Until that person tells you,
You're not the one they want.
But where was the love that should've lasted forever.

Memories of the past you had of the future,
Memories of time, time that has now passed by.
But where was the love that should've lasted forever.

Tragic deceitful lying love that was meant forever,
Fighting that grew larger, stronger and harder.
But where was the love that should've lasted forever.

The clock is ticking,
They are now the foe.
Your lifelong feeling is no longer a vow.
Hear the cries of whistled fury.
Their short-term affair so silent and heartbreaking.
But where was the love that should've lasted forever.

You had your life so little and fair.
Where was your conscience it was never bared.
Adultery may be a simple word,
Just think of the partner that you betrayed so unfair.

Kimberley Hamilton (12)
Summerhill School

DIANA

The country mourns Diana,
An angel, a princess.
In fact not just a country -
The world is in distress.

She was so very precious in,
So very many ways.
We're all so very angry at,
The way she ended her days.

Someone soon must think of,
A way to end the drink and drive.
If it weren't for these irresponsible people,
Many more would be alive.

She will be loved forever,
Bathing in the fame.
The terrible way she lost her life,
Isn't it a shame.

Diana you were a gem,
You were like a rose in bloom.
You have left us numb and weak,
Among the gloom and doom.

You were one of God's best,
A radiant English rose.
And like no other gone before,
This is the way they chose.

Britain has lost the jewel in the crown of its Royal Family.

Louise Hickman (13)
Summerhill School

THE BALLAD OF MY HOLIDAY

I went on holiday,
It was a fine day,
The sea was cool,
I knew I would enjoy my stay.

I was playing on the beach,
The sun was hot,
The fair was there,
And I won a lot.

The motel was good,
The swimming was brill,
I jumped in the deep end,
It gave me a thrill.

I went to three shows,
They were really funny,
I sat three rows from the front,
It didn't cost too much money.

On Tuesday morning,
I went on a boat,
All kitted out,
Up the river I did float.

I played a game of crazy golf,
I got a hole in one,
Lost against my Dad,
Won against my Mom.

No more clothes left,
Time to go home,
I got in the car,
Oh did I groan.

Mark Hancocks (12)
Summerhill School

GOD'S GIFT

Is this world a place in which you want to live
With pollution, sky-rises and the rest?
CFCs and sprays destroying the ozone layer,
Is this the world at its best?

Smoke and fog or even smog,
Is this what we really want?
People killing trees and plants,
P'haps we can stop it p'haps we can't.

Oil rigs, dumps and slag heaps,
Waste in the sea and on the land,
And who is suffering? Us.
Is that something grand?

Greenpeace, peace and war,
Drawing weapons like before,
But this time they are different weapons,
Are we coming to death's door?

Save the Earth for our children,
Save it for the future,
So they'll save others after them,
When they become more mature.

Is this world such a burden,
Or is it such a pleasure?
For this is God's Gift,
He has given us forever.

David Owen (12)
Summerhill School

TALES OF ALIENS

Some aliens have antennae
And funny pointed ears
Some tall, some thin, some doll-like
Some live for many years.

Silver spaceships shaped like saucers
Or long, round, fat cigars
Are used by many aliens
To get from here to Mars.

Some aliens are very kind
And wish no harm to you
But some are very dangerous
With faces that are blue.

But how to recognise between
The good and evil ones
Is more than the colour of
Their faces or their tongues.

Communications what you need
When meeting folks like these
They may not understand a smile
They may prefer a sneeze.

So if one dark and scary night
An alien you meet
Don't wait around or you might be
His favourite kind of meat.

Sarah Croft (12)
Summerhill School

GAINING

'T-minus 30 minutes,' the speaker announced,
The five lucky astronauts waited,
The lines on their faces were very pronounced,
For this was their first mission.

They edged to the platform upon which the shuttle stood,
This was something they'd wanted to do,
But had always thought they never would,
For this was their first mission.

They sat inside the shuttle Gaining,
The latest one from NASA,
They reflected upon months spent training,
For this was their first mission.

With a loud roar the engine ignited,
The shuttle began to shudder,
The astronauts felt extremely delighted,
For this was their first mission.

They burst through the atmosphere and out into space,
And took up an orbit around Earth,
Like many before them from their race,
For this was their first mission.

All of a sudden a loud alarm sounded,
The shuttle spun out of control,
On hearing all they immediately floundered,
For this was their first mission.

As they hurled towards their demise,
A ruptured fuel tank leaked,
The tears welled-up in their swollen eyes,
For this was their last mission.

Amy Macklin (12)
Summerhill School

BRIDGEWATERS!

On the 19th September in '73,
A boy called Carl hit a tragedy.
His full name was Carl Bridgewater,
He lost his life to a murderer.

> He was a 13 year old newspaper lad,
> The person who shot him must be mad.
> They were there to do a robbery,
> And they were nicknamed the Bridgewater three.

He was shot in a house on the A449,
The thought of dying never crossed his mind,
He was found in a house on Yew Tree Farm,
When he was discovered it was quite an alarm.

> The police and ambulances rushed to the scene,
> An horrific sight they'd never before seen.
> They found some silver and some crockery,
> Down a lane not far from Wordsley.

The Bridgewater three must have been mean,
At first they denied ever being there at the scene.
They were found guilty by the fingerprint men,
They couldn't deny anything then.

> They were sent down for twenty years,
> But the parents of Carl still live in fears . . .
> They still believe it was those three men,
> The memory of Carl will die with them.

The Bridgewater three after their eighth appeal
All sat down to a freedom meal,
After serving eighteen years,
The parents of Carl are still weeping tears.

Claire Thomas (12)
Summerhill School

THE PIED PIPER OF HAMLIN

One day a stranger came to town,
The little town of Hamlin,
Saying that he was really smart,
With his wee whistle of tin.

To rid them of their problem big,
Rats had come to live with them
The mayor he spoke to the new stranger,
While he ate a brulee of creme.

He did as he said,
And the rats went in the water.
The stranger came for his fee,
The mayor said 'No,' and laughed like a snorter.

The piper was angry
His face grew red.
His mind schemed for a way to get back,
He thought hard, he thought strong, the idea popped in his head.

'Twas such a saddening day,
He lead them to a mountain cave
Where all the kiddies went away
And they were never to return.

All the children, 'cept lame Hans,
Who couldn't keep up with the rush.
He didn't make into the piper's hands,
He said the music promised so much.

'Twas the day that Hamlin mourned,
For all their dear little children.
Who were never seen again,
They ended up in the piper's den.

Danielle Curtis (12)
Summerhill School

Vesuvius Disaster

In the far-off land of Italy,
There was a dormant volcano disaster,
It came without warning,
But no one believed,
It would be a most tragic disaster.

In the town of Pompeii,
One morning it came,
As a lump in the middle of the land,
But even as it grew no one could believe,
It would be a most tragic disaster.

After a while the lump had stopped moving,
And nobody thought anything of it,
But it laid in wait,
And waited for when
It could be a most tragic disaster.

And then it did happen,
Out of the blue it came
And smoke poured out of its cone,
Rocks flung themselves at the vulnerable town,
That would be the scene for its tragic disaster.

At last Pompeii knew,
It was time for alarm,
But alas! It was too late,
For the lava gave no mercy for the people of
The town of the tragic disaster.

When all was ended it was a terrible sight,
As smouldering ash lay everywhere,
And the villagers stood like statues,
But for tourists who go there every year,
It is the town of the tragic disaster.

Mary-Kate Thornton (12)
Summerhill School

A Trip To London

The coach arrived,
We all got on
Ready to travel
Down to London.

        The journey was long
        We had a laugh
        We stopped at Windsor
        At a cafe.

We got to the hotel
And then we were roomed
That was the day
London was doomed.

        Forty or more
        Rowdy school kids
        Crossing the roads
        Making cars skid.

The theatre they visited
Pizzaland too,
More drinks were ordered
And there were queues for the loo.

        The night on the camp bed
        Meant I couldn't rest,
        The weather was so hot
        I slept in pants and a vest.

On the way home
We played Beetle Slap,
The water snake burst
Over a girl's lap!

Ben Cole (12)
Summerhill School

THE GALLANT HEDGEHOG

We sing of the Gallant Hedgehog
The greatest of them all
Was just a tiny little thing
Just seven inches tall.

It was on a little walk one day
Just after the cock had crowed
The hedgehog family came upon
A very busy road!

They're not going to get us this time
They said grinding to a halt,
For we have brought along with us
This super catapult!

'No way,' said one,
'Do you think I'm mad?'
'I have a life you know,
But as I am the father, I'll have to have a go!'

He climbed aboard
They fired him off
But they all felt really sorry
Although he cleared all the cars
He never made the lorry!

They said, 'We'll do it next time!'
We really really must
We won't end up like road-kill
'Cos another one bit the dust!

So that's the story of the Gallant Hedgehog
A sorry one I know
The catapult's still there today
Come along . . . and have a go!

Nick Capewell (13)
Summerhill School

A Ballad Of Pollution

Ships spill oil into the sea,
And they really shouldn't be
Poisoning the ozone every day,
In the end we'll all pay.

Litter, smoke, fumes and oil,
Rubbish from houses poisoning the soil.
Poisoning the ozone every day,
In the end we'll all pay.

We must recycle, there's no time to wait,
Because if we don't it'll be too late.
Poisoning the ozone every day,
In the end we'll all pay.

People on protest because they care,
They're all helping and we just stare.
Poisoning the ozone every day,
In the end we'll all pay.

We're polluting our Earth,
It has to be said,
And if we don't do something we'll end up dead!
Poisoning the ozone every day,
In the end we'll all pay.

Sarah Foster (12)
Summerhill School

BALLAD OF TELEVISION

Neighbours, Home and Away, EastEnders too,
Different choices for me and you,
So many programmes for you to see,
So much fun watching TV.

Never get bored from watching all day,
Go with TV and don't delay,
So many programmes for you to see,
So much fun watching TV.

All the channels one, two, three, four,
If you have cable there are a lot more,
So many programmes for you to see,
So much fun watching TV.

Now coming out is the new Channel Five,
With programmes recorded and programmes live,
So many programmes for you to see,
So much fun watching TV.

Cybil, Frasier and even Friends,
Never a dull moment, never the end,
So many programmes for you to see,
So much fun watching TV.

Drama, comedy and then a cartoon,
Lots of programmes from dusk, dawn to noon.
So many programmes for you to see,
So much fun watching TV.

Emma Osbourn (13)
Summerhill School

MY THOUGHTS OF 31ST AUGUST

The driver was three times over the limit
But he didn't care,
But after he crashed the Mercedes-Benz,
He's have wished he wasn't there.

The paparazzi chased the car
Where they saw Diana and Dodi
They wanted to get a picture of them
That one was an oldie.

Dodi was pronounced dead at the scene
But Diana wasn't dead
The doctors rushed to save her life
They put her in a private bed.

The doctors tried to massage her heart
After it had stopped beating
Then the doctors pronounced Diana was dead
They confirmed it with a meeting.

The newspapers changed their headlines
Even though they hadn't the story
The writing so big that it filled the page
It had no pictures they were too gory.

So England had lost the 'English Rose'
Everyone was sad
Everyone felt for Diana's sons
This thing for them was so sad.

Matthew Wassell (12)
Summerhill School

THE GHOST OF CAPTAIN MCGRATH

There was a huge waterfall
    and heading in its path,
Was a small pirate ship
    it was Captain McGrath.

He was a sea-tyrant
    the most feared of all,
And he had no idea
    that his boat was soon to fall.

He was cruising along
    in his motorboat,
When lo and behold
    his boat would not float.

For he had come across
    a nasty strip of water,
He was about to die
    it was manslaughter.

Even though he steered and dodged
    and tried his utmost best,
The waterfall claimed his life
    and now he lies in rest.

So if you ever go swimming
    by a massive waterfall,
Beware you might be swimming
    in Captain McGrath's pool.

Ben Packwood (13)
Summerhill School

THE LOST CHILD

Stephen
He was my only child
My pride and joy
The only thing I had
The one me and his mum
Made
Together.

I walk into his room
I don't see my Stephen
All his clothes cluttered on the floor
Strange
It doesn't bother me anymore
I wander through his room
Deep in thought
Trying to find a clue
What did I miss?
This boy I thought was in the safe clearing
Was lost in the dark and lonely wood.

Now
He's gone
Slipped out of my hands
Just like his mother
Is it my fault?
I ask myself
Over and over again
Everyone I've loved
Has left me.

My world's split in two
They've gone to a better place
But me
I'm still here
In this cold and heartless world
Alone
Without Stephen.

Meloney Rodney (13)
Sutton Coldfield Girls' School

THE CIRCUS

Clowns with silly hair and red noses,
Chase around and make everybody laugh.

Ladies in sparkly leotards and bangles,
Prance around on the backs of white horses.

Trapeze artists swing around in the air,
Acting like monkeys, jumping from tree to tree.

Gymnasts cartwheel and flip around the room,
Everybody's eyes dazzle with amazement.

The elephants walk into the ring,
Children scream and reach out to touch them.

The lion roars as its tamer plays with it,
Everyone goes silent and still.

Everybody waves to the circus at it travels along
                                       the road,
Off to go and please somebody else with its
                        spectacular performance

Gemma Soden (11)
Sutton Coldfield Girls' School

TIME'S CRUELTY

Time is the essence I shall never control,
Through its path it has made me smile,
Through its turmoil I have also cried.
In many lifetimes I have sought solace,
In many ways I have lost the peace.
During the cold winds, my flower withers,
During this darkness my candle fails to burn.
Now I no longer need love like I used to,
Now the end is closer than ever before.
Amongst the lost stars I sail into the night,
Amongst several wishes I strive to be a reality.
So I've never seen the truth,
So you've always told the lie,
But now this life is ending,
Show your grace, be not afraid to die.

Nyla Yousuf (16)
Sutton Coldfield Girls' School

A WINDOW VIEW

Looking through the window.
so many things to see.
The world seems to have,
that touch of perfect harmony.

Looking at the deep blue sky,
not any clouds in sight.
It could go on forever,
and yet that can't be right.

The world has that air of mystery,
that seems to never end.
It's as if there's something new,
round every corner bend.

Everything in this world,
has its own special place.
It was created to work,
and yet this, we cannot face.

Looking through the window,
so many things to see.
The world seems to have,
that touch of perfect harmony

Lydia Corbett (14)
Sutton Coldfield Girls' School

TOMB

Of what significance are you and me,
In this grey, dusky, calculated place,
Only living at the turn of a key,
A push of a switch or look on a face.
Mechanical movements, lifeless almost;
Automatic steps, unfeeling it seems,
Delete wonders of which nature can boast,
Where green grass glistens, the gleaming sun beams
And the wildlife croons its innocent tune
As a plea for help or a warning call.
Yet who can deny that silvery moons
Are works of art shared kindly with us all,
Being part of everything good and pure,
Not the grey, sad tomb we have to endure.

Lucy Ray (16)
Sutton Coldfield Girls' School

SOUND AND SIGHTS OF WAR

The sirens like a ghostly howl
blares out at everyone, like a warning from hell.
Panic and chaos has now arrived to a nation of terrified people.

The whirling and wailing of the stuttering engine can now be heard
and is coming nearer and nearer.
The flying beasts are on a mission, carrying their cargo of destruction.
Down below people wondering 'Will I live or will I die?'

Now the dark kings of destruction come rumbling down
shattering the silence and leaving people trembling with fear.
The big black monstrous bomb came smashing down leaving red
and yellow flames, so delicate yet so destructive.

They rustle and rumble monstrously through the land.
Destroying everything one by one.

Silence, deadly silence
The sirens gone, nothing moves in the ashes that was once a town.

Sehreen Riaz (11)
Sutton Coldfield Girls' School

SILENT BULLY

I looked down at the shivering body,
And could see straight away she was new.
I gave her the 'evil eye',
Icicles trickled down her bony face,
Her knobbly knees shattered to pieces.
A silent call for help.

Her meek body carries the load of her bag,
Her uniform and coat added to the pile.
A uniform so perfectly perfect,
Enough to make you sick.

I wasn't like that I'm sure,
As strong as steel I was, (I think),
The sixth formers still frighten me though,
They're a lot, lot bigger than me,
They make me shiver in such a queer way.

Thu Huong Nguyen (13)
Sutton Coldfield Girls' School

HEADMASTER

His stare could bore
right through your heart.
Shattering your spirit
into tiny pieces which could never be repaired.

His stare could find
its way from the back of your head.
To the front,
as if to say,
though you cannot see me, I am still there.

And if you looked into his eyes,
you would find nothing
but coldness and loneliness.
He, a cold and barren place,
which could never have
been touched by warmth.
Where is the man
beneath the stone?
Or where might he have gone?

Gillian Fildes (14)
Sutton Coldfield Girls' School

I Stop And Stare

Walking down the street,
I stop and stare, but no one's there.
Shh! I hear someone call my name.
I turn around,
But still,
No one's there.

I walk down the big streets of Africa,
I stop and stare.
But this time, when I turn around,
Someone is there.
Not a whole someone,
Just a black clothless child.
Suffering,
From malnutrition and other diseases.

Why is it
That when you stop and stare,
The whole world seems to,
Cluster around you?
Why isn't everybody
The same?
Because everyone in the whole world,
Needs the same kind of
Love, care and happiness.
The same kind of love, care and happiness
You and I get,
Everyday of our lives.

Rupinder Kalsi (13)
The High Arcal School

PLANTS

Roses, daffodils, bluebells too,
Red, yellow, green or blue.

Thin, fat, short or tall,
Some even climb up the wall.

The plants need watering every day,
Or they will just wither away.

Some grow from cuttings, bulbs or seeds,
What you don't want, are those weeds.

Plants need to survive, the rain the sun,
Growing plants is really fun.

Growing plants takes a lot of time,
But the end result makes you sing
a little rhyme.

Laura Rudd (11)
The High Arcal School

INDUCTION WEEK

I start a new school tomorrow.
My heart is in my throat.
Moving from class to class.
I'm sure to get lost.
I'm definitely going to get lost.
I start a new school tomorrow.
I can't find my stationery.
I call to my mom.
I call to my dad.
It's no good.
I start a new school tomorrow.

Samantha Vanes (11)
The High Arcal School

FIRST DAY BLUES

Mom, where's my trainers?
Mom, where's my bag?
I can tell today is gonna be a real drag.

I can't find my bag
Great! Great! Great!
If I don't hurry up, I'm gonna be late.

I look at my timetable
All the lessons I hate
I hear the school bell go as I rush to the gate.

My friends go through the door
I'm all alone
At times like this I want to go home.

The day ended great
It's the end of the day
I really do like this school and that's where I'll stay.

Vikki Loach (12)
The High Arcal School

DESTRUCTION

Think of a world without any sunshine
Think of a child without any toys
Think of a baby without any mother
Think of a world without any joys
Try and understand the needs of a
Friendship and this world should
Stay alive.

Shelley Haldron (11)
The High Arcal School

THE TEST

I saw the paper coming towards me, I knew I was doomed
The paper dropped before me
I was nervous I'd get less and the others would get more.
And they would laugh at me forever more.
The questions were running around in my head.
Would they be hard or easy instead.
And then I heard the teacher say, start
And my jumping heart pounded more

I walked out of the hall, the breeze hit my face
The test was all over at last
But it kept running through my head
Would I get more or would I get less.

Jenna Grainger (12)
The High Arcal School

THE BLACK COUNTRY

In the black country we speak with
a very rare lingo.
You can hear it in shops, pubs and bingo.
Yo cor and I wow are really just the norm.
The kids start to learn it from the day they
were born.
It's unique, it's special it leaves all
in its wake.
I'm proud of the black country and the way
that we spake.

John Humphries (13)
The High Arcal School

MY MOTHER CALLED TO ME

I was sitting on the garden wall
I didn't hear my mother call
Come now, come now she said aloud
Your grandpa and your grandma have come around
Come on, come on, come get your tea
You'll be surprised at what you see
I walked through the door
My head was bowing to the floor
Oh dear, of dear
A present for me
What is it, I thought
I'll open it and see
I opened it
A bike for me
Oh grandpa and grandma
Just look at me
Oh grandpa and grandma
Thank you, oh so dearly.

Sarah Louise Marsh (12)
The High Arcal School

HARVEST

H is for the hay the farmers gather.
A is for the rosy, red apples we pick.
R is for the reverend who says all the prayers.
V is for the vases of flowers we display on that special day.
E is for the eggs that the chickens lay.
S is for the special services we go to on Harvest Day.
T is for tomorrow that follows that special day.

Now we can't wait for the next Harvest Day.

Michelle Jones (11)
The High Arcal School

PUNCTUATION

Nouns and pronouns,
Do you know what they are?
You put them in sentences,
And your writing'll go far!

Punctuation is what you need,
To make sense of what you read!

Full-stops and capital letters,
Do you know what they are?
You put them in sentences,
To show where the breaks are.

Punctuation is what you need,
To make sense of what you read!

Question marks
Do you know what they are?
You put them in sentences,
To ask what the questions are.

Punctuation is what you need,
To make sense of what you read!

Lydia Rodgers (11)
The High Arcal School

GRAMMAR

Grammar is for English.
As we all know
A simple sentence has
one verb,
eg, the man was
so low.
The verb is the man
as you all should
know.
A simple sentence
is its name, I
think it goes like
this.
A man walked over
the park and then
into his house.
If you read this poem
you will find it
might say a lot of
things but none of this
is true.

Oliver Watchorn (14)
The High Arcal School

FOOTBALL

Have you ever seen a football match?
They're such a lot of fun,
the fun that is good and clean and nice.

I went to a football match yesterday,
this is what I saw.

People jumping up and down,
because a ball went in a net.

I got squashed like a big orange.
A man in a black T-shirt and a pair
of shorts, shouts orders.

Then a big fight starts.
A colossal mass of coloured shirts.
Then the crowd join in.
Isn't football weird.

Scott Evans (11)
The High Arcal School

SCHOOL

Schools, schools
All have their rules
Don't run in the corridors or in the labs
The smell of chalk as you walk in the classroom
The smell of Bunsen burners as you walk in the labs
The playground covered in litter
The sound of children as they bicker
Children ticked off as classroom lights flicker
Isn't it great to be at school.

Marc Skeldon (13)
The High Arcal School

MY HAMSTER

Oscar is my hamster
he keeps me awake all night
he lives in my bedroom
he lives in a purple cage with
a purple wheel and a purple house
I think he likes purple
he tries to climb up his cage
he is a very cunning hamster
he is always running around

When he is hungry, he sits in his food dish
and eats his food
after that he starts again
he's like a little scamp
Oscar is my hamster
and I love him loads.

Helen Harris (13)
The High Arcal School

I'D RATHER BE

Blue

I'd rather be red than blue.
I'd rather be boots than a shoe.
I'd rather be me than who.
I'd rather be me than you.
I'd rather be false than true.
I'd rather be in front than in the queue.
I'd rather be human than a shrew.
I'd rather be iron than brew.

Wayne Grose (12)
The High Arcal School

WINTER

The snow is on the ground.
The snowflakes are in the air.
Christmas around the corner,
Can't wait will I get out there.
Hooray I'm out there.
I think I'll build a snowman,
Why not, I've got the time.
I need a scarf, a hat, a carrot,
And oh yes, currants for the buttons.
The children have red noses,
They look like strawberry splits.
I think I'll go in for the hot chocolate now.
I'll move the cat from the fire.
Why not, I'm cold
Whoops,
Bump,
Slippy floor.

Susan Howell (13)
The High Arcal School

I'D RATHER BE

I'd rather be red than blue
I'd rather be a neigh than a moo
I'd rather be me than you
I'd rather be a drink than a chew
I'd rather be a trainer than a shoe
I'd rather be a whistle than a boo
I'd rather be lazy than do
I'd rather be where, than who.

Rachel Wildman (12)
The High Arcal School

THE HABIT OF MY CAT!

Big cats, little cats,
Fat cats, thin cats,
Cute cats, ugly cats,
Ginger cats, black cats,
White cats, tortoiseshell cats,
When she's been out at night,
She stalks like a bird of prey,
She runs like a lion and growls like a fox,
She runs like a squirrel, and scrapes like a dog,
She sits like an elegant lady,
And stands like an ox,
In the day she lies content in the sun,
At night she's alert for prey on the run,
In the morning she returns ready for food,
I watch my beautiful cat, full and purring as
She sits washing,
In a contented mood.

Laura Gibbons (12)
The Streetly School

STREETLY SCHOOL

When I started at Streetly.
I thought the dinners would be completely yuk!
And the teachers would be horrible

But I couldn't believe my luck - the teachers
are quite tolerable,
And the dinners are tasty - but hang-on let's
not get too hasty,
Oh well, time will tell.

Naomi Smith (11)
The Streetly School

NORBERT CHEESEWRIGHT

Norbert Cheesewright smells like egg,
Sometimes I do really beg,
For Norb to put deodorant on,
But when I turn around Norbert's gone.

I look for Norbert in the park,
He says, 'I'm playing Noah's ark.'
'Noah's ark?' I say to him.
Then he goes and hides in the bin,
'It smells in there,' I say to Norb,
Then he gets out his magic orb.
'Oh no, oh no, don't do it Norb,
Please don't wave your magic orb.'
'Don't be silly of course I won't
Especially now you said don't.'

The very next day Norbert left,
He said he was heading for the planet Cweft.

Thomas Folan (11)
The Streetly School

THERE'S A HOLE IN MY SOCK

There's a hole in my sock
It's our washing machine
It's eating our clothes
Not washing them clean.

It's swallowed some pants
We can't open the door
It's bubbling out soapsuds
All over the floor.

Thomas Cole (11)
The Streetly School

School

I don't want to do games sir
My mom's brought in a note
I've got a broken leg, sir
Please look at what she wrote.
Is maths really useful?
Do we need so many lessons.
I can't take all the numbers,
In Monday to Friday sessions,
Un, deux, trois, quatre, cinq, sir,
  1   2   3   4   5
Nudge me in the side, sir,
Am I still alive!
I've got to write a poem sir,
Just little old me,
Who do you think I am, sir
The poet Laurie Lee,
Did Van Gogh have art lessons, sir?
Did he have to go to school?
Did he have to start with plants, sir?
I feel such a fool!
But if I want to be on TV!
Prime minister of the country,
I suppose a few more lessons will,
Make a smarter me!

Luke Crawford (11)
The Streetly School

My First Days

My very first day I came into the world,
A flurry of excitement and joy,
It was a world so different from mine.

My first ever holiday,
Down by the sea,
It was an experience so different from home.

My first day at nursery,
I cried for my mom,
It was so different to be on my own.

My first day at school,
I was only five,
It was so different to be here full-time.

My first day at the comp,
Was full of worries and thrills
It is a life so different from the one that I knew.

Sarah Underwood (11)
The Streetly School

Motor Racing

I like motor racing,
It is really fast,
I like to watch the motor cars,
Racing past.

I go to meetings with my dad,
My cousin Stephen, too,
I wish I was a driver,
Or part of a Formula 1 crew.

I like to go to Silverstone,
Donington Park, too,
The GT's are really fast,
All of them old and new.

Some people go to camp there,
Others come on the day,
To watch the racing cars,
Racing away.

Richard Bignell (11)
The Streetly School

WINTER

I like winter because . . .
the snow is here
It is fun and we all
make snowmen and have
snow fights.

I like winter because . . .
the wind blows
in your face and
your cheeks go
bright red.

I like winter because . . .
the leaves fall off the trees
and when you walk under
a tree the leaves crunch underfoot.
Winter is just fun.

William Willis (11)
The Streetly School

AT THE ZOO

I went to the zoo today,
On one fine day in May,
I saw lots of animals there,
Some even gave me a scare,
Especially the grizzly bear,
I saw a big fat monkey jumping up and down,
Smiling at a boar with a big fat frown,
The lion moved around, looking very mean,
So I fed him my brother,
Which he chewed like a bean.

The elephants grew so jealous,
I gave them a shoe to chew,
The giraffe was struggling with a crow,
Who wanted a fight,
But we set him a flight.

I can't wait to visit the zoo tomorrow,
There's so much for me to go and see,
I'll visit the lion's roaring den,
And the piranha's sparkly pen.

I love the zoo!

Victoria King (11)
The Streetly School

TEENAGERS

At the age of thirteen,
You are called ignorant and mean,
By your father and mother,
These accusations they discover.

They don't understand,
That it wasn't all planned,
For us to behave like this,
They thought it would all be bliss.

We all start to fight,
It's not an uncommon sight,
We all push and shove,
Then, fall in love.

With the boy down the road,
Or the girl from the club called the 'Load',
Those beautiful eyes,
Who cares if he or she lies.

He's dating six others,
Or she's fallen out with her mother,
There's always a disaster,
When you're a teenage master.

Then all is calm again,
The child is sane again,
The parents can relax,
Until their younger son Max . . .
Turns thirteen.

Eleanor Jones (13)
The Streetly School

JESSIE BROWN

There was a girl called Jessie Brown,
And she was the hottest cowgirl in town,
Her guns are always strapped to her leg,
They're even there when she goes to bed.

She has curly brown hair and beautiful blue eyes,
They're almost as big as lemon-meringue pies.
She's tall and thin and very well known,
And she likes to eat ice-cream cones.

She has very strange eating habits, the strangest
I've ever seen,
For example, she eats chocolate covered octopus,
With baked beans.
And for a drink (now this isn't quite as strange)
Chocolate and strawberry milkshake with bits of
Sugar cane.

When the bad guys are in town, they start to tremble
                                       with fear,
Because they know if Jessie Brown is near.
She's the best shot in town, wins every time,
Every bet she places, she wins every dime.

Well now it's time to say goodbye,
Because Jessie can get quite shy.
But don't you worry because Jessie will be back,
To fight all those bad guys who start to attack!

Chevon Morgan (11)
The Streetly School

5TH NOVEMBER

It's here. It's here!
The 5th of November is here.
When you look out on the night,
You'll see the fireworks high and bright.
There's rockets, Catherine wheels and
others too.
Why don't you try a few.
Catherine wheels spin round and round,
But they are not very loud.
Rocket shoot up in the sky,
Some of them go very high.
Put a banger on the ground,
This is a firework that bangs
very loud.
Fireworks that go round and round,
Listen carefully to the sound.
When rockets bang and fireworks
crack.
You must take care to stand well
back.
For when it's over, we all shout,
'Please don't put the fire out.'

Hayley Aston (11)
The Streetly School

SCHOOL

School is terrible when you're in year seven,
Teachers talk and imagine it like heaven.
But oh are they wrong,
In music you have to sing a *song!*
And Mr Maybury,
Well he teaches Geography,
Mr Coxedge teaches art,
And all the teachers think they're smart.
I even try to tell my mum,
But she thinks I'm dumb,
That I really, really hate school.
There's even no water in the swimming pool.
Now you know a bit of this,
I think I'll give school dinners a miss.
Now you know a bit of my school,
Don't you think it's really cruel?

Christopher Westwood (11)
The Streetly School

FOOTBALL, FOOTBALL

Football, football is the best,
It's a better sport than all the rest.
Aston Villa are my team,
because they are the best ever seen.
We watch the villa run around,
and run the other team into the ground.
When they score, you hear us roar,
and bang our feet upon the floor.

Laura Eadon (11)
The Streetly School

IN THE MORNING

I wake up at six, my eyes are red
Even though Mum's shouting,
I try to stay in bed.
First one foot, then the other,
But I keep thinking, where's my brother?
He runs up the stairs then and
pulls my hair,
But I don't hit him because I care.
We run down the stairs, my brother and me.
We both sit there till we've had some tea.
We eat toast, all cereal we can choose
Then we get ready to go to school.

Danielle Clarke (11)
The Streetly School

OH DEAR

Cheep, cheep, chatter, chatter,
My two budgies, make such a clatter.
Chirrup, chirrup, squawk, squawk,
How on earth can I do my work?

Dogs are barking, woof, woof, woof,
Brother playing football, he looks a scruff.
Sister playing music, mum washing-up,
Please be quiet, so I can read this book.

This house is so noisy, such a din,
It'll be worse when Dad gets in.
The telephone rings, oh I must leave home,
On second thoughts, I couldn't live alone.

Elize Bevan (11)
The Streetly School

DIFFERENCES

Different culture, language and races
Different times in different places.

Different beliefs all with different views
Which makes all the conflict on the news.
Different countries, but in a world that's one
All the wars and fighting should have gone.

People walking at such a different pace
But all are competing in the same race.
People trying to win their own game
When everyone in the world should be playing
                                       the same.

People think they're different because of a name
But the real truth is that we're not different -
                                     but the same.

Joanna Hall (13)
The Streetly School

ABOUT ME

Collette is my name.
Oh, netball is my game.
Lizards I do like.
Like riding on my bike.
England are my favourite team.
Though when it comes to playing, I'm not very keen.
Things like books and magazines.
Every day I like to read.

Collette Tomkins (11)
The Streetly School

A Day Of My Life

Got up one morning out of bed,
Shook the sleep from my weary head,
Into the bathroom then I go,
To have a wash nice and slow,

Down the stairs then I stumble,
As my stomach starts to grumble,
Breakfast cereals just waiting for me,
Toast and jam and a nice cup of tea,

Off to school then I go,
Meeting friends walking slow,
Through the school gate then I walk,
To my classroom where teacher talks,

Into assembly for hymns and prayers,
Then to my first lesson down the stairs,
About the pollution and the planets,
Art is the next lesson where we use paint palettes,

Dinner bell rings throughout the school,
Time to pack away our woodwork tools,
Nosily, chatting eating lunch,
Dinner ladies shouting at the noisy bunch,

Lunchtime over all too soon,
Back to lessons for the afternoon,
Home time eagerly awaits for us,
Then a big rush for the homeward bus.

Aaron Acton (11)
The Streetly School

MY DOG *BEN!*

His nose is cold,
and his eyes are sad.
He's simply the best friend,
I've ever had.

He loves to play,
and run in the park,
and when he gets excited,
he will bark and bark.

He jumps on my bed in the morning,
He likes to chew my shoes,
and even when he's naughty,
There's only one dog I'd choose!

Ben my little friend!

Allanah Marsham (11)
The Streetly School

THERE'S A MOUSE IN THE KITCHEN

There's a mouse in the kitchen
Playing skittles with the beans
He's drinking cups of tea,
And eating last year's cheese.

There's a mouse in the kitchen,
He's eating tomorrow's dinner.
But at least he's washed the dishes.

Katie Gettings (11)
The Streetly School

THE FOOTBALL FAN

I am an ardent football fan,
And I watch it when they play.
You always hope your team will win,
But it doesn't work that way.

Last year my team was doing well,
They were 4th in the Premier side.
The fans were keen and cheered them loud,
And wore their kit with pride.

But this season they are slipping,
They have lost their winning touch,
Everyone of us is worried,
We don't like it very much.

We've lost a couple of new players,
Replaced by someone new.
They need some time to settle down,
Then we'll see what they can do.

But this week things are looking up,
It really was a thrill.
They played away at Yorkshire,
And beat them 3-nil.

So now we'll cheer them loudly,
And try to show we care,
And if they manage to reach the top,
Our support will keep them there.

Alex Wetton (11)
The Streetly School

AUTUMN

Summer's faded and autumn's here,
The air's gone cooler,
The sky's gone clear.
The woodland's changing from green to gold,
The animals are preparing for the winter's cold.
Squirrels collect their winter store,
And hide it outside their own front door.
The leaves are falling to the ground,
A crunchy carpet all around,
The animals hear every sound.
Acorns and conkers fall from the trees,
Helped along by the autumn breeze.
Soon the trees will all be bare,
And Jack Frost will be in the air.

Sarah-Jane Lloyd (13)
The Streetly School

CATS

Grey, black, tortoiseshell and white,
Asleep in the day but most active at night,
The mouse in its hole trembles with dread,
And hopes that the cat has already fed,
The pads of its paws make not a sound,
As the cat makes its move and circles the ground,
The squeal of the mouse does not fill
half the house,
As the light draws in he forgets these affairs,
Once again she is the sweet little cat
            who sleeps on the stairs.

Kelly Craddock (11)
The Streetly School

WEATHER

The weather is hot sun shining through
The ponds, lakes and rivers are a shimmering blue
The bees and wasps are flying up high
Aeroplanes gliding away in the sky.
But now the summer's over, autumn is on its way
We'll miss the summer, we wish it could stay.

The days get shorter, the nights grow cold,
The ground is covered with colours of red, bronze and gold.
The smell of autumn is in the air
The trees and bushes turn completely bare
The crisp early morning, with dew on the ground
No hedgehogs, squirrels or rabbits are found.

With winter on its way, damp misty and grey
In winter woollens wrapped up tight
The children now have a snowball fight.
The foggy mist strangles the air
The layer of snow which in summer is rare.

Now the days are warmer, and the nights are longer
The April showers, blossom, the flowers
Chickens hatch, the lambs are born
The grass is growing on our lawn
The weather changes within the seasons
And I like them all for different reasons.

Mark Carmichael (11)
The Streetly School

SCHOOL

I get up in the morning ready for school,
And pack my bag with papers and ruler,
I walk out the door and through the gate,
And down the road to meet my mate.

At school my worst day has got to be,
Monday or Tuesday, then on Friday we're free,
I've made lots of new friends whom I sit by
in class.
We play in the playground and on the grass.

My best lesson is French but I like science
as well,
I always rush outside when I hear the bell.
And now it's home time, I've had a great day
at school,
The next day I'll pack my bag, pencils and
ruler.

Elizabeth Sealey (11)
The Streetly School

THE CD ROM

As I was going to the park,
I met a dragon in the dark,
I stuck a sword right through its neck
Blew it up, made it a wreck,
What's that shouting? Oh, it's mom,
Better switch off the CD ROM.

Catherine Patterson (11)
The Streetly School

HARVEY MY HAMSTER

Harvey is my hamster,
Who's cute, fluffy and clean,
He loves to go to sleep all day,
And he is very tame, not mean.

He loves to wander on the floor,
But we don't know where he goes,
Once he went behind the fireplace,
And came out with a black nose.

He loves all kinds of little treats,
Cucumber, apple, carrot and cheese,
He cleans after every meal,
And does not have any fleas.

He has a sandy-coloured fur,
And has white marks in many a place,
He has small hands and feet you know,
And has a gorgeous face.

So Harvey, he is really sweet,
And won't bite you at all,
I love him very dearly,
Now he is off in his ball.

Holly Dugmore (11)
The Streetly School

FOOTBALL

Everyone's ready for the game,
The players are trembling in the changing rooms,
The stadium fills up one by one
The fans start to roar when the players come out of the tunnel.

The game is off and the ball's spinning fast,
The referee has blown his whistle,
All because it is a foul,
The fans are going crazy.

The half-time whistle has blown again,
The players are back out and play,
The team is on the attack,
The player shoots, the team scores.

There are 90 minutes on the board,
The referee is about to blow,
The whistle has blown for full-time
The fans are cheering out loud.

I'm really happy that we have won,
We were the better team,
We were stronger, bigger and better.

Adam Whitehead (11)
The Streetly School

THE THEME PARK

Here is the roller-coaster whizzing
round the track.
Here it comes again
going clickety clack.

Here is the ghost train
Oh no! I'm really scared!
No way am I going on it!
And that's what Mom declared.

Here are the bumper cars
They go really fast
Then all of a sudden
My brother came flying past.

It's the waltzers!
This is my last ride
Then I will go home
I'm really really tired.

James Kimberley (11)
The Streetly School

THE SEASONS

Autumn is here at last
Leaves are falling from the trees
Changing colour from green to brown
Swirling around in the gentle breeze.

Winter is here at last
The trees are bare and the flowers have gone
Snow is falling all around
Children have built many snowmen, not just one.

Spring is here at last
Lambs are being born
Flowers are beginning to grow
The trees are new and not so worn.

Summer is here at last,
The sun is out and it's very hot
The birds are singing and the bees are humming
Flowers are in bloom, there are quite a lot.

Sally Peel (13)
The Streetly School

SISTERS

Sisters are weird things,
Always happy and merry.
They bounce around,
Their feet never touch the ground,
Until their eyes feel heavy.

They wake up in the morning with all the joys of spring,
They go to school all happy to see what the day will bring.
When it comes to lunch she feels a little glum,
When it comes to home time she feels rather dumb.

When she comes home she runs into my room.
To find me getting changed.
I shout and shout until I am red,
So she runs downstairs and tells our mom
                        I was off my head.

Paul Morris (13)
The Streetly School

PARENTS

I love my parents, I'm sure you do too.
The only thing is they're annoying
They worry and fuss especially when we're hurt
But they are always fully alert.

They like the house all clean, neat and tidy.
But this is where we come in.
We keep it in a very big mess,
And give our parents lots of stress.

Chantel Reynolds (11)
The Streetly School

POEM PROBLEM

I think and think of what to write,
How do you write a poem? I say,
What topic? What style?
Please tell me, if you may.

I'll start off with a rhyming poem,
But one word just won't rhyme,
Should I leave it and carry on,
My head tells me that's a crime.

So I start again, a different poem
This time it's about people's looks,
But now I've got no more ideas,
I know! I'll look in some books.

Books haven't any ideas,
So I decide to cheat,
I'll write a poem I wrote before,
But I can't, I've got cold feet.

So here I am, writing one now,
Got no problems in this poem.
Look at me, I've nearly finished,
Except the last line doesn't rhyme.

Amritpal Thiara (13)
The Streetly School

My New School

The first day of school is drawing near.
I'm not sure whether to feel happiness,
sadness, hope or fear.
What will people think of me
with my grey pleated skirt down to my knee?
New teachers, friends, books and more.
Detentions, referrals, I have never
had one before.
Last year I was the oldest in the school.
I am just going to be standing there
looking like a fool.
I am just trying to think to myself,
there will be other people like you
who are nervous and want to make
a friend or two.

Hannah Motzheim (13)
The Streetly School

The Lion

The lion runs around the jungle looking for his prey,
He finds something to pick on,
And pounces right away.

After his lunch he drifts to sleep whilst thinking what to do.
He wakes up with a start,
He dreamt he was locked in a zoo,
He got very sick of people saying,
I feel so sorry for you.

Sophie Nuttall (13)
The Streetly School

A Fishy Tale

A whale swam on the sea,
And saw a sailing ship,
The ship he saw was sinking,
And the captain bit his lip.

As the ship was going down,
The crew jumped off the sides,
The whale swam to save them,
But they were washed in by the tides.

The crew swam to the beach,
But the captain wasn't there,
He was still on the ship,
Combing his thin hair.

The captain peered into his 'scope,
And shouted to the shore,
'You abandoned ship too quickly,
The ship ain't sinking anymore.'

The crew waded into the sea,
And shouted to the whale,
'Please give us a lift to our ship,
Or the captain will put us in jail.'

As the crew and whale neared the ship,
The captain clenched his fist,
'The next time you abandon ship,
To jail I will insist.'

The first mate turned to the crew,
And said, 'We'll return to ground,'
And whispered in the whale's ear,
'Oh mate! Just turn around.'

Gemma Alexander (14)
The Streetly School

THE FLUFF

The fluff that sits in the bottom corner
behind my bed.
Why does it choose to drape itself above
the cobweb which highlights the worn-away varnish?
And what lingers in the crevice where paint and
vanish meet?

The story goes that in Tibet a butterfly spreads
its wings,
And though its wings may not span an inch a
hurricane it brings.
And so the piece of fluff in the corner insignificant
and small,
May not be so insignificant in the end after all.

Richard Wellings (13)
The Streetly School

PRINCESS DIANA

Princess Di loved the world,
She treated it like a pearl,
Landmines and bombs she had no fear,
She never exited at the rear,
Her boys she thought the world of,
She never saw them married off,
Which is a shame because she had
so much life inside her,
Grandchildren would be loved
so dearly by her,
She will be sadly missed by everyone.

Jade Thomason (13)
The Streetly School

MY POEM

Write a poem the teacher said
A poem about what?

What have I done?
Who have I seen?
Who do I know?
Where have I been?

I stared at a blank page
I bit my pen.

What makes me cry?
Who do I want to be?
What do I find funny?
What annoys me?

Still no ideas
I'm racking my brain.

Where do I live?
What do I eat?
What do I love?
Who will I meet?

I bet Carol's written a good one.
I'll just copy hers.

Judith Buckley (13)
The Streetly School

PEACE?

Sometimes when I sit and think,
I wonder for a while,
If only there'd be no more wars,
That thought would make me smile.

If men would put their guns away,
If knives and bombs were banned,
If landmines disappeared from sight,
We'd have a happier land.

I go on to think what it'd be like,
If disease no longer spread,
If all the homeless had a home,
And all the starving were fed.

If only people would stop and think,
Then all these things may cease,
And love was given to everyone,
Our world would be full of *peace*.

Kim Mills (13)
The Streetly School

DOLPHINS

The dolphin jumps, high through the air,
The dolphin dives, people stand and stare.
The dolphin bounces a ball to the crowd,
The people stand and cheer very loud,
The ball is thrown, giving reflections
                from the sun
Soon this performance will be over and done,
So the dolphins leave, diving all the way,
And now they will wait for another day.

Aaron Rhodes (13)
The Streetly School

AUTUMN

Autumn comes with a gust of wind,
Around lie its crispy leaves.
Swaying trees of orange fire,
Swept by the soft cool breeze.

On the grass the dew rests fresh,
Children with rosy cheeks.
In the morning the sun beams down,
From behind a cloud it peeps.

Shadows lengthen as the nights
draw in,
Stars have a silvery glow.
Animals hurry for a place to sleep,
Next day the strong winds will blow.

Rosalind Jones (13)
The Streetly School

TELEVISION

A television isn't just for programmes,
There's more to it than meets the eye,
It's a box of information whose intelligence is high.
It's an alien in the corner, with an aerial on its head,
It's got a big square body and legs made out of lead,
It's a spaceship that's just landed in your living room,
It's brown and black with shades of grey,
But I'll still watch it every day.

Gary Bailey (13)
The Streetly School

THE BULLY

Big and strong he stands so tall,
His looks enough to frighten all,
Piggy eyes so dark and cruel,
He doesn't need another tool.

His voice so loud, his breath doth reek,
Victims are such easy meat,
One raised hand, an ugly look,
Followed by a big right hook.

No one dares to stand his ground,
They are not prepared to stand around,
One loud shout his word is law,
Opponents never come back for more.

Sean Davies (13)
The Streetly School

FLYING

Oh dear, I really do hate flying
I feel like I am dying
I can taste the sick at the back of my throat
The guy sitting next to me is gonna get soaked
Blergh!
Oh dear all over the floor
Why is everyone moving towards the door?
Those lumps look like cheese
Oh and those, like peas!
I do hate it when this happens
It's so embarrassing
Especially when we haven't even taken off yet!

David Underwood (13)
The Streetly School

THE VICTIM

She hurts her more,
than a fist ever could.
She's so confused,
like a bomb killing innocent people,
or a war that,
should never have begun.

She's so scared,
but worried that the torture
will never stop.
She wants to tell her to stop
but isn't brave enough.

No one hears her pain.
In her mind,
she's hating her friends for not helping,
but knows they can't help,
for like herself they are scared.

Hear her voice,
She pretends she is deaf,
blocking out the teasing.
When will the taunting stop?
Hear her voice!

Rebecca Floyd (13)
The Streetly School

Diana

Diana you're the moon, the sun, sea and sky,
You were the golden teardrop in my eye.

Diana you're that lantern that lit my darkest street,
You gave me strength when I was weak.

Diana you're the jewel I'll cherish forever,
You were the sparkling gold that I kept in my treasure.

Diana you're the sun that dried the rain away,
You're in my heart and that's where you'll stay.

Diana you're the scent of a fresh flower,
You added to my life so much power.

Diana you're the idol that I wanted to be,
You gave me my eyes when I couldn't see.

Diana, you're the angel sent from above,
You gave this to the world so much love.

You're part of God's family,
And you'll never be released.
We all miss you Diana, so,
> *Rest in Peace!*

Sarah Neale (13)
The Streetly School

ALL SORTS OF WEATHER

The weather is good,
the weather is bad,
and when it starts to rain
I feel so sad.

The sun is yellow
the sky is blue
If you see a lightning cloud,
it might just hit you.

The snow is cold
the beach is hot,
and when it's just right,
I like it a lot.

When I get in
from out in the snow
I get myself warmed up
and back out I go.

It rained all day
it snowed all night
and when it started lightning
it gave me such a fright.

Then along comes autumn
and the leaves fall off
it gets so cold,
you get a nasty cough.

Gary Chandler (12)
Willingsworth High School

The Ghoul

If you stay awake at night,
You will see a gruesome sight
Before you can scream he takes you away
Over the hills and far away.

When he takes you in his cave
He doesn't expect you to behave
You try to escape through the door
With one slash, you're no more!

His eyes are red
With spikes on his head
So boys and girls don't think it's cool
To make fun of this ghoul,
And when you're tucked up in your bed
Just think it's good to be alive
       and not dead!

David Evans (12)
Willingsworth High School

Parents Moaning

Have you washed your face?
Have you washed your feet,
Don't forget to feed the dog,
And give it some meat.

Do you know what a hoover is,
Do you know how to clean?
If you don't,
I might get mean.

Go to bed,
You rotten boy,
If you don't
You might cry.

Hurry up and brush your teeth,
Hurry up and wash your feet,
Hurry up and get to bed,
Goodnight sweetheart, *my little ted.*

Stephanie Brookes (12)
Willingsworth High School

CASPER MY FRIENDLY RABBIT

Casper my white rabbit
Had a very bad habit.
He chewed his paw
Until it was sore.
With water we did dab it.

He was fluffy and cream.
Looked at you in a dream.
She messed with my books.
Gave you looks.

PS
Casper died 12.10.97
A fox bit her head off
between 7 and 8am
and buried her in my rockery.

Paul Powell (12)
Willingsworth High School

My Cat

My cat Kiri is so sweet.
Pointy white paws she has, so neat.
Creamy white fur, oh so glossy,
Sometimes she can be quite bossy.

My cat Kiri is a little bit fat,
But I don't care *'cause* she's my cat.
I was scared of her
But now she's my best sister.

I love to watch her as she purrs.
She treats my bed like it is hers.
And with cute little paws
She scratches on the doors.

Hayley Jones (11)
Willingsworth High School

Moving House

I'm moving into my new house,
I looked into my room I saw a mouse
The garden was a horrible mess
I looked on next door's garden and saw Jess.
Smoky our dog, was pouncing on me
Then my cousins came Jason and Ste'
Then we watched Coronation Street
Then we gave them a treat.
They came upstairs and played games
Mother came in she said 'What a shame!'
All the mess I made
I thought it was the trade
I fussed the dog up
But he is only a pup.

Christopher Anslow (12)
Willingsworth High School

I Wonder!

(Written by a girl in the 22nd century who wonders what a 'giant panda' would look like. Sadly she'll never know as it's estimated that by the 22nd century, all the world's pandas will have died out.)

I look at the thing,
That is sitting in the corner,
It looks rather sad,
Its head lopped over to one side.
I begin to feel sorry for the thing,
So I walk over and pick it up,
I stare at it sadly,
And it seems to stare back.

I notice how large his eyes are,
They seem marble-like,
They also seem deep and sad.
Then I notice its large paws,
They're just a little smaller than my hands,
I look at the colour of his paws and arms,
They're black right up to his shoulders,
His legs are just the same.
I notice how large its body is,
It's nearly as big as me,
And then I notice how soft its fur is,
Or is it that soft because the thing is not real?

I sit down in the chair,
The thing is too big for me to hold much longer,
As I look at it I realise it must be a 'giant panda',
My dad is always telling me about.
It's a real shame they are extinct,
And then I wonder what it would have been like,
To see a gentle giant, the *'panda'*.

Sarah Edwards (11)
Willingsworth High School

The Shuffle

I was walking in the woods to
visit my grandma.
I heard a shuffle in the bush
I ignored it
The noise wouldn't stop
I was curious
I walked quicker
I started to run
It chased me
It was only a rabbit
I left my grandma's house
I heard a noise again
This time I wasn't curious
I turned round
There it was a creature from beyond!

Shaun Burton (12)
Willingsworth High School

Sisters

Sisters can be sisters,
Sisters can be twins,
Sisters always argue,
Until one always wins.

Sisters go around together,
Sometimes they don't,
They sometimes shop together,
But sometimes they won't.

Sisters squabble, sisters fight,
Until their mother shouts,
'Stop that banging,' then goes
And gives them a clout.

Sisters can be sisters,
Sisters can be twins,
Sisters always argue,
Until one always wins.

Rachel Arnold (12)
Willingsworth High Sc hool

FOOTBALL

Football is a game
Where you have to use your
Brain.
You use your voice
But you can't be nice.
You have to tackle
And battle for the ball.
When you get injured
And get tackled hard,
You have to go into hospital
And people will send you a
Card.
You have to use your wit
But football keeps you fit.
The game is very demanding
I like it when I win.
Football is very good
You get to fall in the mud.

Dean Birch (13)
Willingsworth High School

MAGIC

Black magic, white magic, yellow magic, blue
They are all fun and all for you.
Black magic, grey magic, brown and green
Evil magic, magic unseen
Magic, magic everywhere
In the walls and in that chair
Magic, magic, it's sometimes fun
It's in that ice-cream van,
    hurry, hurry, hurry, run, run, run!
Wizards, witches and warlocks
    they know the trade
So come along, don't be afraid!
Grab your cloak and ride that broom
You know it's never too soon . . .

Jonathan Hancock (13)
Willingsworth High School

MY FAVOURITE FOOD

Chocolate, ice-cream, cake and jelly,
All these things I love in my belly,
I love to eat my favourite foods,
I'd eat them all day long,
Even though they're bad for me,
And I know that it's wrong.

Sometimes when I'm hungry,
I sneak a chocolate bar,
I eat it in my bedroom
And hide the wrapper
        in a jar.

Laura Evans (11)
Willingsworth High School

SHOPPING

When I go shopping with my mates
It's nearly all the time we walk past the iron gates.
On the way we talk and talk
We get off the bus and start to walk.
When we are there we go to McDonald's
And we sometimes meet Ronald McDonald.
But sometimes we just don't eat
And sometimes I have to go and get meat
Just for my mom and dad to eat.
We go in the Sports shops and buy some
trainers or we just don't buy anything.
Then off to the music shops to buy some tunes
I wanted this album but it doesn't come
                            out till June.
We come out of the shops and look everywhere.
There are no people, the shopping centre's bare.

Lee West (13)
Willingsworth High School

MY FAVOURITE SUBJECT IS

English is my favourite subject,
I hate maths,
But I love English,
I hate history
But I love English
Science is okay
But I love English,
I like music, it's great,
But I like English best of all
    because we have Mrs Mumford.

Tara Houldey (11)
Willingsworth High School

Hallowe'en

It's Hallowe'en soon
Watch out for the ghosts
Don't be frightened and don't
be scared.

They're coming to get you
They will definitely come
There might be a lot or
might only be some.

Ghosts are scary
I'm telling you so
don't run away,
        don't go!

If you hear a knock on the door
and you're eating your tea
don't answer the door
you never know what it might be!

Vicky Martin (13)
Willingsworth High School

When I Started Willingsworth

When I first started Willingsworth High,
It all seemed very strange.
I couldn't believe how different it was,
But I liked the change.

The teachers were very nice,
The food was definitely top,
Once I'd seem to have started,
It was time to stop.

We had maths and French,
On that same day.
'You will have me for this subject,'
The teacher started to say.

The food was great,
The lessons were cool.
I would never go anywhere,
Other than Willingsworth High School.

Jane Kirkham (11)
Willingsworth High School

THE WITCH'S SPELL

Lion's heart, dragon's scale,
Human liver, whale's tail,
Baby's foot, ginger cat,
And a wing of the African bat.
Round and round my cauldron go
Make my pets grow and grow.

Meerkat's eye, boy's hair
Child's blood, nose of bear,
An adult's finger, elephant's tusk,
And lots of dirt and dust.
Round and round my cauldron go,
Make pets grow and grow.

Cow's leg, dog's throat,
Tail of tiger, teeth of goat,
Claws of falcon, beak of a platypus
Asleep in the dust.
Round and round my cauldron go
Make my pets grow and grow.

Alison Joiner (12)
Willingsworth High School

A Nightingale

A bird called Nightingale
Was always black and white
Children called him Flightingale
Because he flew.

A bird called Nightingale,
Had sparkling green eyes
Babies called him Blewinbale
Because they could not say Nightingale.

A bird called Nightingale
Had great big wings
Teenagers called him Lightingale
Because he shone in the light.

A bird called Nightingale
Had feathers the size of . . .
But not many people called him Tightingale
Because of tight and large feathers.

A bird called Nightingale
Was always black and white
Everyone eventually called him Nightingale
Because he flew in the night.

Rebecca Hartshorn (12)
Willingsworth High School

SCHOOL

School, school, are all schools
the same, do they all have silly rules
Like no food fighting?
The best part of the day is 10 past 3
when the bell goes *ring!*

The school dinners are yuk,
They taste like muck,
The custard is thick
And the potatoes are as hard as a brick!

Lessons are long
And the classrooms pong
You sit there for hours wondering when
Miss will ask you to put down your pen.

Being shouted at is bad,
Because after your telling off comes detention,
Oh drat!
Here comes Mr Ridley, attention!

School is bad,
Worse than my dad,
So bewarned don't come,
Because teachers wait for you to put one
foot wrong so they can shout.
(not true of course.)

Nicholas Slym (12)
Willingsworth High School

THE TRAMP

He is lonely
He is sad
He is cold
He is so bad
That it's likely he would get better
And nobody ever, ever sent him a letter.

He lives on the edge of the street
He rummages through the bins
And he has nobody to meet
So he tries to find some tins
He has got smelly feet
And he tries very, very hard to get something to eat.

Craig Ratcliffe (13)
Willingsworth High School

GIBBETS LANE

It was a gloomy night.
I saw a ghost in the trees.
It said 'Come and hang with me.'
I turned to run then I stopped.
And there was a stream of dark
                      red blood.
Running from the stream,
I heard a strumming sound.
I saw an illuminated light
It was so bright it blinded me.
I was by a house, it was my house.
But it was still a spooky night.

Stacey Farmer (11)
Willingsworth High School

THE GHOST

I sat in silence waiting for him to come.
But he never turned up.
He came every other night about 12pm
He was tall, handsome and very young
He had dark wavy hair and blue sparkling eyes.
He wore Victorian clothes and looked
as though he had no dress sense at all.
I wonder where he's gone,
He usually walks past me when I am
sitting quietly in the dark,
I don't think he ever noticed me,
He just walks slowly through the
front room and down the stairs.
I do hope he comes back soon
I will miss him.

Aimee Noone (13)
Willingsworth High School

THE GRAVEYARD HORRORS

Graves everywhere
While playing with my pear.
Graves here and there
While I hide with a scare.
Graves all around
A very spooky sound
My friends come around
I crawl on the ground.
I jump with a scare, with a *boo*
They run with a scare
Then they were aware
      that something was there.

Paul Shaw (12)
Willingsworth High School

My Hamster, My Hamster

My hamster, my hamster, living in his cage,
My hamster, my hamster, running with rage.

My hamster, my hamster, he loves his food,
My hamster, my hamster, I play with him
               when I'm in a good mood.

My hamster, my hamster, Ozzie is his name,
My hamster, my hamster, lets you hold him
               he's tame.

My hamster, my hamster, his colour is grey,
My hamster, my hamster, he sleeps all day.

My hamster, my hamster, I hardly see him out,
My hamster, my hamster, loves a drop of stout.

My hamster, my hamster, what a cheeky face
               he's got,
My hamster, my hamster, I love him a lot!

Ross Griffiths   (11)
Willingsworth High School

Children

On Hallowe'en in Hall Lane
Quite close to the city shops
The children lit a bonfire
And the adults called the cops

Disgusting minds sing nasty songs
And speak in dreary prose
While others make home-made bombs.
One of the hostages was really hot
And her face lit up like a rose.

Some say it was the UVF
Some say the IRA
Blew up that little city
And killed the kids at play.

Perhaps they didn't mean the children
It might have been the blast
We call it 'Kill the Children Day'
In little old Belfast.

Natasha Hickman (13)
Willingsworth High School

SCHOOL! SCHOOL!

School, school, is the best
But sometimes you just need a rest
Some lessons I really hate
So I try to be really late.

Teacher gives us homework and
Everybody sighs
When it comes to hand it in
Everybody lies.

Lunch bell rings
It's time for lunch
Quick, let's hurry
It's time to munch!

Next lesson I really adore
I wish we had it more and more.

Now I have got to go
Next time I see you
I'll say 'Hello.'

Thomas Hayward (12)
Willingsworth High School

MAGICAT

I could swear my cat Magi is magic,
She can play a guitar and make us say hooray.
She can jump from roof to roof and
we don't need proof.
She's as fast as the next and she'll
beat the rest.
She's a pyscho killer hooligan gorilla.
She's on automatic and a telly addict.

My cat Magi is a silly-billy girl.
Silly-billy girl she may be but she's a 'Magicat'
and a 'Magicat' she is.

I could swear my cat is magic, she's a 'Magicat'.
She will eat a Mars and then jump to Mars.
She's a smelly cat and a fat-bellied cat.
She wears a pair of Nike air shoes that rule
               but after all she's a *Magicat!'*

Brian Wright (13)
Willingsworth High School

RAINBOW

It's breezy today, dull and wet
We haven't seen any sunshine yet.
But when we do I'm sure it will be
Just through those dark clouds,
Over there, see!

When the rain stops
There is bound to be
A *rainbow* joining the
Sky to the sea.

Michelle Howes (11)
Willingsworth High School

HALLOWE'EN

Hallowe'en here once more
Children knocking on my door
Trick or treat
Dressing up
Getting money in a cup.

Hallowe'en is a fun year
We love to fright,
And love to cheer.
Oh what a night
We had last night.

We're having a good time
Especially me
Everybody enjoys it,
Nervously.

It's been good
So far so good
Trick or treat I want a sweet
Come on in and take a seat
I can't come in my Momma said
I've got to be in for four and go to bed

Hallowe'en, Hallowe'en
I love it so much
Hallowe'en, Hallowe'en
It's got a special touch.

Nicola Shaw (13)
Willingsworth High School

MANCHESTER UNITED

Man United are the ones for me.
Keane, Giggs, the best of all.
Man United are . . .
Kings of the ball.

Floodlights are on.
The whistle is blown.
90 minutes from now
We'll be wearing the crown.

We're on our way home,
We've done it again.
What a team, these eleven men!

Hello! We're back again.
Still supporting these skilful men.

Remember remember this brilliant team
'Cause we're 'The Reds'
D'you know what I mean?

John Flavell (11)
Willingsworth High School

FRIENDS

I know it was very wrong of me
I definitely must admit
When all my friends offered friendship
I called them all a twit.

I didn't want anybody else,
To come hang around with me,
At least I have my best friend left,
So she had to choose between me and the rest.

The boy I loved was no longer there,
I had no one to care,
All my friends came to me,
They said 'How stupid can you be?'

Me and my best friend had a fight
It turned out that she was right
I went and found all my friends
And know all our friendships
               will never end.

Lynsey Arnold (14)
Willingsworth High School

THE NIGH OF THE 31ST OF OCTOBER

The 31st of October has arrived,
witches and ghosts come alive,
witches flying in the air,
Mum, it's not fair, I wish I could
fly through the air.
Long hair, pointed nose,
and also very big smelly toes.
There was a ghost as clear as a bell,
all he did was tell,
then his Mum had had enough
and started to yell.
There was a mummy,
who sucked her dummy,
and tickled her tummy all the time.
She thought she was funny,
until she lost her money
and that was the end of the old mummy.

Laura Cartwright (11)
Willingsworth High School

MY NAN

My Nan she's one of a kind
If I ever do something wrong she'd smack my behind
She'll join in with me, if there's any fun
All of my family will, except for my Mum.

She sits there watching the telly
Or is in the kitchen making her favourite jelly.
My Nan thinks that she is rare
And she just sits there on her comfy chair.

My Nan just thinks about how she's turned out
She doesn't like noise, or people running about.
Well life's life and I don't waste my time
I wonder what it's like doing a crime.

My Nan now she's the one
Who knows how to get things really done
If I want something like some cash
My Nan will give it me, she's always got
                          some stashed.

My Nan thinks my mates are great and they like her too,
Do you ever wonder about your Nan, 'cos I do.
But as a friend you were the best
      but as a Nan you beat the rest.

Tracey McFarlane (14)
Willingsworth High School

OUR STREET

Parents and children always together,
Inside and outside depending on weather.
In our street it's lots of fun
In the summer with games for everyone.

Football, netball and golfers too,
We always find something to do.
Parents sitting by the garden gate,
Laughing, drinking till really late.

When it gets dark we don't care,
The spotlight's come on and we sit in the glare.
It lights up the garden and half the street.
The kids carry on with running feet.

When the winter comes the kids play out
When mealtimes come the parents shout,
'Come on now it's time to eat.'
Now there's no one in our street.

In the winter it all seems still
All night we're in with time to kill,
But when it snows, it's so cold we don't care.
The snowballing starts and we're soon out there.

Beryl Evans (13)
Willingsworth High School

BIRTHDAY

It was my birthday
It came once again
It only comes once every year
I wish it could be twice
Or three times perhaps.
This year I only got a teddy
Other kids get more.
Maybe that's why three birthdays
Would be good,
Or I got more and they got less.
My sister got a cake
And my brother went to McDonald's.
My Dad gets everything from my Mum.
It's probably the same with every kid.
The smallest get less.

Ben Pearce (12)
Willingsworth High School

THE TROLL

Be wary of the loathsome troll,
That slyly lies in wait,
To drag you to his dingy hole,
And put you on his plate.

His blood is black and boiling hot,
He gurgles ghastly groans,
He'll cook you in his dinner pot,
Your skin, your flesh, your bones.

He'll catch your arms and clutch your legs,
And grind you to a pulp,
Then swallow you like scrambled eggs,
Gobble! Gobble! Gulp!

So watch your step when you next go,
Upon a pleasant stroll,
Or you might end up in the pot below,
As supper for the troll.

Rachael Jones (13)
Willingsworth High School

SWEEP AND TIGGER

Sweep and Tigger were just good friends
Playing and rolling in the fields
Chasing cats and climbing trees
Until one day they got caught by the breeze

Over the hills they did roam
Cold, hungry and missing home
Tigger saw a familiar figure
So Sweep followed him close
Afraid to lose all hope
Sweep still close on Tigger's paws
Following Tigger, following the figure.

Around the corner they did pounce
Seeing both their monsters
Faster and faster they did run
To the warmth of their homes.
Will they wander away from home
Over the hills forever to roam . . .

Lee Kendall (11)
Willingsworth High School

A Witch's Brew

Heart of deer, tongue of rat,
Eye of newt, cow's fat,
Liver of dog, wool of lamb,
Now let's add in a quarter of ham,
Woman's voice, dead man's lips,
Sister dear, fetch his hip,
Toe of frog, lizard's leg,
Noise of sea, rotten egg,
Nose of pig, jaw of shark,
Arms of children from the park,
Now stir it thick and stir it thin,
Now put it in a baked bean tin,
Double, double, toil and trouble,
      watch the water bubble!

Samantha Capewell (11)
Willingsworth High School

A Witch's Brew

Brain of baby, devil's guts,
Turkey's liver, rabbit's wings,
Angels' chorus, reindeer's rage,
Slug's slime, bat's ears
Kiddies' toes, eye of frog
Belly of rat, dead dog's eyes.

'Mix it thick, mix it thin'
Put them in a garbage bin!

Paul Holl & Gavin Woodhouse (12)
Willingsworth High School

WITCHES' BREW

Eye of Medusa, wing of bag,
Spear tip of native, claw of cat,
Ear of dog, an ounce of green slime,
Lizard spit and small fraction of time.

Around the cauldron we will dance,
To the devil's boiling prance,
So let us do this dance one more time,
Before the tower clock strikes nine.

Three feathers of goose, tail of a dog,
Egg of quail, bark off log,
Front teeth of T-Rex, stripe of tiger,
Smell of dingo plus brain of spider.

Sarah Edwards & Kay Humphries (11)
Willingsworth High School

THE WITCH'S BREW

Leg of dog, leg of mouse
Put it in a wizard's house

Wing of bat, tail of horse
Make it with a spell of course.

Stir it thick, stir it thin,
Make it with a bit of win.

Tiger's howl, bat's wing
Pig's bottom, bird's ping

Stone of rabbit, stone of bat
Put it in a hazard's hat.

Stacey Evans (11)
Willingsworth High School

GHOSTS

Ghosts where do they live
I wonder
Under the stairs perhaps
Or under your bed?
They could be hiding in your
Wardrobe ready to pounce at any time.
Are they nice or are they evil
Nobody knows, nobody cares
Because of course they're make-believe.

Or are they?

Maybe one might jump up from under your bed
And swallow you whole.
But of course they can't because they're make-believe.

Vicki Bentley (12)
Willingsworth High School

UNTITLED

A dark and gloomy night
Something gave us a fright
When we were walking through the graveyard
Late one night.
The squeak of the bats and the
Scream of the cats
When the stray dogs prowl
And the hoot of an owl.
As we were running through
I tripped and lost my shoe
Then I looked around and a
                        man said *'Boo!'*

Matthew Rudge (12)
Willingsworth High School

HALLOWE'EN

Children trick or treating
  people running off
pumpkins moving, everyone
  screaming.

There's mums and dads
  trick or treating
aren't they a bit too old
  but children are scared
    ghosts are coming

Brothers and sisters
  having a good time
but everyone's
  scared to go to bed tonight!

Terri Steventon (12)
Willingsworth High School

WITCHES

The day the witches came out,
They put a spell on me,
What sort of spell could it be,
I've got this tingly feeling inside,
And I just can't get it out of my mind,
But since then I could:
Make fires with my eyes
Look at a boy until he cries,
I can put things in the air
And I fly in the air,
I have never ever saw the witches again,
But they might come back to visit again.

Sarah Martin (11)
Willingsworth High School

KATIE

Today we had a baby
we named her Katie
she is a pain
but we love her so much.
Every time we put her down,
she always cries for Mum.
When I go to hold her
she cries some more.
Gran comes round every day
to see how her little flower pot's
getting on.
Me and Grandad sit there
having a drink and a chat
we let the women get on with their
job and that's the end of that.

Nathan Smart (12)
Willingsworth High School

A BEAUTIFUL ROSE

A beautiful rose of misty blue,
With purple spider webbed patterns too.
With a fragrant scent that rises high
The tall blue rose is set against the sky.

The perfumed scent fills the air
And sends its beauty everywhere.
It is opening more into a charming flower
And gaining more beauty every hour.

A charming blue as pale as the sky
Still gaining beauty as it grows so high.
It thrives on the rain and grows in the sun
For me to see and everyone.

It keeps on growing until the day
When its beautiful colour fades away.
The rose gradually starts to die,
Then on the ground the rose will lie . . .

Zoe Patel (12)
Willingsworth High School

THE SAD DOG

There was a dog
her name was Sandy
she was always sad and lonely.

She went to bed and had a nap
on the kitchen floor.
She woke up at half-past two
to have some food.

She had some food
for five minutes.
She went to play outside.
She found some friends
to play with and she was
happy again.

Samantha Steventon (12)
Willingsworth High School

I Wonder

Sometimes when I'm all alone
I sit and wonder
what if . . .
I flew to the moon,
landed on Mars
sat there in darkness
and counted the stars.
Swam a deep sea
with its bottle-blue waves,
went out exploring inside hidden caves,
fought in a war,
Oh I've thought that before!
Or maybe just nothing at all.
Stuck in a desert
with nothing to drink.
Those are the things
I like to think.
So I wonder sometimes
when nobody knows,
full of ideas, bursting
inside my head,
got to break free,
those are ideas that I've just said.

Samantha Richards (12)
Willingsworth High School

HALLOWE'EN

There was a witch
who had a cat
who once went out
and ate a rat.

There was a vampire
in the sky with a bat
on a magic mat.

There was a mummy
who sucked a dummy
when she went on a fright
in the middle of the night.

There was a witch
who caught a fish
out of the sea
then she ate it
for her tea.

There was once
a boy witch
who played football
on a pitch,
and like any other boy
he had a favourite toy,
but unlike a normal boy
his favourite toy was
a dead rattlesnake,
which he ate with a piece of cake.

Stephanie Dicken (11)
Willingsworth High School

THE SPELL THAT WENT WRONG

A bit of this and a bit of that
We'll soon have it done
He'll be a rat or a mouse, a frog or even an ant
My cat will devour him if he's a mouse
Or a rat
It's done, now for that victim!
Is he here, or over there?
No he's there.
1, 2, 3 oh no he won't change, I will
Aaaaggghhh, I'm a mouse
My cat will devour me now
Miaow, he looks nice
He's coming, help!
Bye, bye!

Jarrad Cole (11)
Willingsworth High School

MY SPORTS POEM

I like gymnastics because it is fun.
I like to show off in front of my Mum.
I like the splits, and tumbling too.
I like the Y-balance but that's hard to do.
I go to Earl's Gymnastics Club.
We are all friends, we all have good fun.
But we do remember the safety rules too,
'Cause being hurt, is no fun that's for sure.
So warm up first up down, in out, phew!
'Cause that's what gymnastics is all about.

Rebecca Vaughan (11)
Willingsworth High School

WITCHES AND BLACK CATS

Witches and black cats,
Rabbits from top hats,
With a magic wand,
Turn the frog in the pond,

It's the 5th November,
A weird night to remember,
Candles in pumpkins,
Spuds in their skins.

The bonfires ready,
Hold the rockets steady,
Because five days after,
There will be loads of laughter.

Leanne Edmunds (11)
Willingsworth High School

MY FAVOURITE ANIMAL

My favourite animal is a cheetah
He likes cheating
At cards
He always cheats at darts.

He's very fast
But a zebra is too fast
For him
He eats lions and lions eat him.

Cheetahs' feet stink
But he loves to skate on an ice rink.

The poem must end
The cheetah eats the end.

Tommy Silvester (11)
Willingsworth High School

THE ROYAL ROSE

The Royal Rose is beginning to open.
The small bud all green is bursting
to reveal a secret.
It opens to reveal a pale pink rose.
The pale pink coat the bud wears
Belonging to the Royal Rose family.
The Princess rose is guarded by prickly thorns.
The thorns protecting the rose are sharp edged
and are warning you off the rose they protect.
But the rose now red as it rises to Queen
lures you in by its sweet scent that pulls you in
and its deep rich crimson red which is a deeper
colour than blood.
But still the thorny guards are there to protect
their Queen from being plucked by the hands of a human.
Then comes the rich deep green of the glossy leaves
that provide shelter from the harsh weather to the thorns.
Then you go to pluck it from its strong green stem
but the thorny guards stop you.
They cut you and you retreat never again
to disturb that Royal Rose.

Jonelle Harvey (11)
Willingsworth High School

KIDNAPPED - HELP

Hidden in the cell,
Waiting for someone to come and rescue me,
In a big maisonette.
They've thrown away the key.

Scared out of my bones,
Don't know what to do,
Waiting for someone to rescue me,
Want to go to the loo.

Then out of the darkness,
I looked on the floor,
Found a glowing key,
And it opened the door.

I ran out of the door,
And I ran home,
Opened the door,
I was all alone.

A minute later,
My Mum came,
She had some chocolate,
She gave me some.

Laura Paskin (11)
Willingsworth High School

My Dog

I have a little dog
Who always needs the bog
He sits on a log
And stares at a frog.

His name is Zak
And he can't quite get the knack
Of sleeping on his own mat
So when he is good
I give him a pat
But when he is bad he chases a cat.

When I take him for a run
He always seems to follow the sun
When the sun goes down
He always seems to have a frown.

Jodie Stanford (11)
Willingsworth High School

Emma The Hamster

She is very active,
She escapes from her ball,
But in the end we find her,
She is always ready to run,
And prepared to hide,
She does not take *no* for an answer,
And Emma gets anywhere,
Once she got behind the washer.

Paul Aston (11)
Willingsworth High School

MY DOG

My dog runs everywhere
Up the stairs,
Down the stairs,
She runs everywhere.

My dog bites everything
She bites my shoes
She bites my slippers
She bites everything.

My dog barks at everyone
At the postman,
At the cat,
At anyone who's there.

My dog plays football.
We kick the ball in the garden,
We kick the ball in the park,
Then she really barks.

My dog sleeps everywhere,
She sleeps by the fire,
She sleeps on the rug,
She sleeps everywhere.

Natasha Collins (11)
Willingsworth High School

PETS

Pets really do make a mess,
And it seems like they never rest,
Except for when's best,
And some live in a nests,
And they really are pests.

I've got a pet dog who chews up vests,
But I still love him
And a pet hamster who chews socks,
But I still love him.
Do you think pets are a mess? Yes.

My pet dog sits on a log he never
Moves until we tell him to.
He chews my papers and my shoes,
He's a bad piece of news,
He's a little rat and hates cats.

My dog is as thick as a log.

Stacey Whiles (11)
Willingsworth High School

SHEBA

When Sheba was a puppy,
She was very, very mucky,
She ate The Daily Post,
Then she pinched my buttered toast.

She was small,
Then she grew tall,
She became hairy,
She became scary.

Her teeth grew sharp,
And so did her bark,
But soon she became a full-grown dog,
Then she tried to eat a log.

When Sheba was a full-grown dog,
She ate my pet frog,
She ate my buttered toast,
Then she would eat The Daily Post.

Laura Powell (11)
Willingsworth High School

WITCH'S BREW

Eye of dog, dead man's toe
Light the fire off we go
Rotten egg, toad spit
Cut off the head of a blue tit.
Spirit of cat, salt from a shark's belly
Plus some frogspawn that feels like jelly.
Tongue of rat, tail of mouse
All things weird in this strange house.
Put in the spoon, stir it well,
Throw in another spell.

Rotten rabbit, with a terrible smell,
With a flame from the fires of hell.
Dog's liver, blades of grass,
Then a few pieces of broken glass.
The spell is finished, just one more thing
We need sounds of bells ringing.
Put in the spoon, stir it well
Throw in another spell.

Craig Jones & Adam Rudge (11)
Willingsworth High School

My Dad

My Dad's taller than your Dad,
My Dad's shorter than yours.

My Dad's thinner than your Dad,
My Dad's fatter than yours.

My Dad's heavier than your Dad,
My Dad's lighter than yours.

My Dad's got more hair than your Dad,
My Dad's got none at all.

My Dad's funnier than your Dad,
My Dad's boring.

My Dad is better than your Dad.

Gareth Berrow (12)
Willingsworth High School

My Canary

I have got a canary
With a bright luminous coat.
His eyes are as black as night,
With nails as sharp as knives.
His coat of feathers is such bright colours
It hurts your eyes.
To catch him you would have to trap him,
For he is as fast as a cat.
He is such a lovely bird,
I'm glad he is my own
To keep and love.

Shaun Hobday (12)
Willingsworth High School

MY FAMILY

My family is made of three,
Including me,
My Mum, Dad and me,
Are three.

But really our family is five
Because two pets are alive
Scruffy the hamster
And Jessica rabbit with her grey fur.

We live in a house,
Without a mouse,
My Mum cooks
And reads books.

My Dad mends and fixes,
And eats Twixs.
We all go out,
And about.

My family is nice,
Like sugar and spice,
And all things nice.
My family.

Laura Amy Saunders (11)
Willingsworth High School

My Family

Every morning is mayhem,
Where's my tie?
Where's my shoe?
Where's my other sock?

Feed the cat
Wash your face,
Brush your teeth,
Clean your room.

Then everyone's gone
But in the afternoon . . .
Fetch your sister
Do your homework
Go to bed!

Amy Hunter (11)
Willingsworth High School

My Dog

My dog ate my favourite poster,
My dog ate my Dad's slippers,
My dog ate my favourite story book,
My dog ate my teddy bear,
My dog ate my pencil case,
My dog ate my hamster,
My dog ate my bike chain,
My dog ate my Dad's CD player,
My dog ate my Mum's new cooker,
My dog ate my PE kit,
My dog ate my homework,
And so my teacher ate him.

Lynseyann Aston (11)
Willingsworth High School

My Father The Fisherman

My Father he goes fishing
he sits alone all day
waiting for that sly old fish
the one that got away.

I make his sandwiches for him
he shares them with his mate.
I know I won't be seeing him
until it's really late.

Then late at night I hear the door go
I think oh no he's back.
I wonder if he's caught that fish
The one he just can't catch,

Nina Howen (11)
Willingsworth High School

My Dog Casper

I've got a little dog his name is Casper
He lives in my house, he goes around
Every morning in my house sniffing on the TV
And on my Mum's bed and in my Dad's shoes
Smelly shoes, smelly socks too.

He has black and brown spots all over his body
He has a little nose to sniff all day long
Outside, inside, everywhere in the world.

He is only four months he bites already
He will be a little bit bigger in five months' time
And bite harder too.
I wonder if Casper has a girlfriend.

Anneka Styles (11)
Willingsworth High School

WITCH'S BREW

Eye of dog, fur of cat
Voice of girl, tongue of bat.
Lizard's leg, pig's fat.

Oil, boil, toil and trouble
Stir it thick stir it in thin.

Lizard's jaw, prickly nail
Monkey's mouth, squid's tail
Elephant's gore, zebra's male.

Oil, boil, toil and trouble
Stir it thick, stir it thin.
Throw it in, throw it in.

Leighanne Pick (11)
Willingsworth High School

MY COCKATIEL LAID AN EGG

My cockatiel laid an egg, I wonder if it hatches,
I wonder if a dinosaur comes out of it,
I wonder if it flies away,
I wonder if it stays,
I wonder if it neighs,
I wonder if it plays,
I wonder if it flies,
I wonder if it cries,
I wonder if it ties,
I wonder if it dies.

Smita Randeria (11)
Willingsworth High School

Why!

Why does he hit me?
Why do I cry?
Does he really love me?
Oh why, oh why, oh why?

One day I will hit him,
Today he's just too big.
I wish I could replace him,
With a little pig.
I love my family
Do they love me?
I can't wait until Christmas comes
Then I can see if they love me.

Samantha Bibb (11)
Willingsworth High School

Sisters

I hate sisters they think they're the best,
But really I think they're such a big pest.

Going around with their thumbs in their mouth,
Really I think they're just a silly mouse.

They hit, they scratch, they punch you too,
We hit them back, they say 'I'm telling Mummy of you.'

Sisters, sisters what are they for?
Being pushy, bossy, being a bore!

After all they are flesh and blood,
I would divorce them all if I could.

Linda Fennell (11)
Willingsworth High School

MY FAMILY

When my sister was born I was really overjoyed,
I felt like killing her because she was so cute,
But after seven years I wished I had done.

My Mum is very nice and kind,
But when I get her mad her eyes look like she's gone blind.

Me, well I'm not so bad, I am very practical,
But when I get mad I am more than very practical,
When I am out with my mates we have a good laugh,
But when we have got nothing to do,
We just sit and kick bricks about.

When my family goes out for the night,
We go to the Karaoke and it's real fun,
My Mum gets drunk and my sister looks like a dork.

Where I live is pretty cool,
I've got loads of friends but,
Most of them are fools,
My computer is my best friend and that's final of all.

Adam Pullen (12)
Willingsworth High School

A Witch's Brew

Heart of deer, tongue of rat,
eye of newt, cow's fat,
liver of dog, wool of lamb,
now let's add in ¼ of ham,
woman's voice, dead man's lip.
Sister dear fetch his hip,
toe of frog, lizard's leg,
noise of sea, rotten egg,
nose of pig, jaw of shark,
arms of children from the park.
Now stir it thick and stir it thin,
now put it in a baked beans' tin.
Double, double toil and trouble,
watch the water boil and bubble.

Zoë Carr (11)
Willingsworth High School

Witch's Brew

Baby's throat, rabbit's blood.
Wool of sheep, cauldron flood.
Tiger's tooth, piece of a baboon's eye.
Dog's tongue, hurry up time shall fly.
Cat's fur, have a quick stir.
Look in the cauldron your eyes go blurred.
Stir it fast, stir it slow
Look how fast the cauldron goes.

Matthew Timms (11)
Willingsworth High School

WHEN I WAS YOUNG

When I was five I thought I'd see
Father Christmas by the Christmas tree.
I'd leave him a nice mince pie,
And he'd leave me a brand new toy.

When I was six I thought I'd see
Fairies come to visit me.
They took the tooth from under my head,
Then left a sixpence there instead.

When I was seven I thought I'd see
The Easter bunny leaving eggs for me.
But I never heard him creep through the door
To leave me Easter eggs galore.

When I was eight I thought I'd see
Father Christmas come down the chimney.
I crept out of bed and looked out the door,
Mum and Dad were putting presents on the floor.

When I was nine I thought I'd see
Fairies take the tooth from me.
But I felt Dad take the tooth from under my head
And Mum left a sixpence there instead.

When I was ten I thought I'd see
The Easter bunny with eggs for me.
But the only eggs that I got
Were the ones Mum brought from the shop.

Kaleigh Garratt (12)
Willingsworth High School

Puddles The Escape Artist

I once had a hamster called Puddles,
who just didn't like her cage,
I tried everything to keep her happy,
but she just wouldn't have it, no way.

One night I crept downstairs,
and opened the door,
to find an empty cage.

I looked everywhere for her but I just couldn't find her.
I looked everywhere, even in the garden.
I went to get a cake when who did I find hiding,
Puddles eating all the cakes.

Samantha Beeston (12)
Willingsworth High School